647.95 H536c   F V
HERBERT
CREATING A SUCCESSFUL RES-
TAURANT : AN EXPERT'S FACT-
FILLED...   14.95

CREATING A SUCCESSFUL RESTAURANT

CREATING A SUCCESSFUL RESTAURANT

An Expert's Fact-Filled Handbook for Anyone Going Into (or Even *Thinking* About Going Into) the Restaurant Business

BY JACK HERBERT

ST. MARTIN'S PRESS/NEW YORK

CREATING A SUCCESSFUL RESTAURANT: AN EXPERT'S FACT-FILLED
HANDBOOK FOR ANYONE GOING INTO (OR EVEN *THINKING* ABOUT
GOING INTO) THE RESTAURANT BUSINESS. Copyright © 1985 by Jack
Herbert. All rights reserved. Printed in the United States of
America. No part of this book may be used or reproduced in any
manner whatsoever without written permission except in the case
of brief quotations embodied in critical articles or reviews. For
information, address St. Martin's Press, 175 Fifth Avenue, New
York, N.Y. 10010.

Illustrations by Janet Tingey

Design by Paolo Pepe

Library of Congress Cataloging in Publication Data

Herbert, Jack.
    Creating a successful restaurant.

    1. Restaurant management.   I. Title.
TX911.3.M27H47   1985   647'.95'068   85–12506
ISBN 0–312–17128–5

First Edition
10 9 8 7 6 5 4 3 2 1

CONTENTS

ACKNOWLEDGMENTS

I wish to express my gratitude and thanks to Alan Fort, for his advice and counsel; Winifred Armstrong, for her encouragement; and to Peter Mehlin, for his suggestions and emendations.

Several other people provided generously of their time and expertise. Special thanks are due to Peter Ray, the White Horse Tavern, New York City; Robert Sullivan, the Customs House Restaurant, New York City; Chris Milano, Lebensfeld Top Equipment Corporation, New York City; and to Nick Bari and Nick Anton of Bari Engineering, New York City.

I am indebted to you all.

J.H.

INTRODUCTION

There are few businesses open to the beginning entrepreneur these days that offer as much personal satisfaction, along with an excellent living, as the restaurant trade. You are to be congratulated on your decision to look into the field. It can prove to be an outstanding investment as well as a thoroughly rewarding career.

The aim of this book is to take you, step by step, from your initial thoughts of becoming a restaurateur all the way to the opening day of your new dining room. In planning and writing the book, I have assumed that your experience in the restaurant field is limited or, even, that it is an entirely new venture for you. As such, you'll need not only guidance but a lot of basic, sleeves-rolled-up information and help all along the way. You'll soon know what you need to know to make the right decisions. I plan to become your *personal* restaurant consultant throughout the book.

We will build your restaurant together. From the moment you first consider a location, through huddles with your contractor, plumber, and electrician, it will be my task to advise you how best to handle most of the problems that will—yes, *will*—arise. The equipment you will require for your kitchen, dining room, dishwashing section, bar, storage area, and office—all this will be discussed in some detail, so that you will know what you're talking about when it comes to ordering your own.

The chapters are progressive, keeping first things first. We will consider factors of proper location and sufficient financing for your venture, for example, before taking up the requirements of heavy equipment and menu pricing. At the back of the book you will find a quick Reference Guide, a comprehensive listing of the equipment and supplies you will need for your new restaurant, as well as licensing and insurance requirements. This guide duplicates for you the individual items discussed at greater length in the main text of the book itself; use it both as a checklist and a reminder. Included in the listing are estimates of probable costs, to give you some idea, in advance, of what you will have to pay for some of your new equipment. Bear in mind, however, as you scan the reference lists, that used and refurbished equipment is often available at *almost half the price of new.* Recommendations in this area, too, are found throughout the book.

The range of greatest profit for most restaurants comes, of course, from the sale of beer, wine, and liquor. Chapter 7 will tell you exactly how to build a bar, what you'll need to install in it, and all the supplies necessary to stock it. Such information is often lacking—or touched upon only briefly—in most restaurant guides.

Now turn the page and settle down for a good read. Keep a pad and pencil handy, and make a lot of notes. That dream restaurant of yours is about to come true.

This is how it's done.

CREATING A
SUCCESSFUL
RESTAURANT

FUNDAMENTALS OF RESTAURANT OWNERSHIP —ARE YOU THE TYPE?

Gregariousness, a sense of showmanship, and a genuine love of working with people are all prime attributes of any successful entrepreneur. There are no shy restaurateurs.

You will be, in an overall sense, the captain of your own ship. As such, like a captain, you will need to know all of the duties of each member of your crew, and be perfectly able to take over for any of them should an emergency occur. This capacity should not only be true in fact, but your employees should be made subtly aware of it as you discuss with each of them the work to be done.

Make yourself at home in the kitchen, and personally cook all the regular dishes that are to appear on your menu. In doing this you will learn the capacities of your kitchen and your equipment as well, and perhaps introduce some changes before you open. Operate the dishwashing machine to make certain that the water is hot enough, the rinse cycle long enough, and that there's room to stack. Offer to bartend in another bar before setting up your own. Waiting tables comes naturally to any outgoing person, but test your own "areas of flow" for the most natural layout, particularly in the pickup area. Learn simple repairs, know the locations of all your valves and outlets, and keep a list of who to call in case of electrical, air-conditioning, or plumbing emergencies. Then you'll be able to sit back, relax, and sew the four gold stripes on the sleeves of your navy-blue jacket. You're ready to *be* the captain.

Not only will you need to come up with correct answers to any of your staff's queries and complaints, but, in time, you should be able to *anticipate* any problems or irregularities. Fear not—just by being on the floor, and attending to all details, you will learn what to do in short order. When you can tell the cook about a problem he's experiencing in your kitchen before he tells *you,* you'll have gained the deference that is your due. And when you solve the problem successfully (and you will), you'll have garnered respect.

None of this is as difficult to accomplish as it may at first sound. When you physically put together your own kitchen, for example, you'll naturally learn not only its capabilities, but its limitations as well. Most restaurant problems are in the area of broken equipment, stalled compressors, clogged pipes, and insufficient heat or air conditioning. Sometimes there's an unexpected run on certain supplies. Since these things—all of them—*will* happen to you at one time or another, be prepared. Learn what makes the compressors hot, and ask your plumber when he installs them to show you how to spot trouble and what to do about it short of calling him. Check your supplies often until you've worked up a routine. Take out a contract for your heating and air-conditioning repairs and maintenance—this will protect you even on week-ends, and is well worth while. When pipes clog, find out why they did, and correct the source of the trouble so it is unlikely to happen again soon. It is, as you can see, a process of trial and error. But as each problem occurs, and is solved, you will be ready to deal with it should it ever crop up again.

Make and keep a list of qualified and accessible me-chanics who can come by to help you when you encounter a problem beyond your capabilities. Keep this list up-dated through the years, and mount it on the wall of your office so your managers will know where to find it if you're not on hand when an emergency occurs.

It frequently happens that an outgoing and gregarious proprietor, for all his or her charm and abilities on the floor and with the staff, is simply rotten when it comes to keeping the books. It's tedious and solitary work—and quite incompatible with showmanship. If this description seems more or less to fit you, then—by *all* means—hire a bookkeeper, at least on a part-time basis, to handle this important part of running your business for you.

If you plan to handle this aspect yourself, your accoun-tant, attorney, or local tax office can tell you what weekly, monthly, quarterly, or annual tax returns you will have to attend to in your location. Be ready to make out *weekly* payroll checks, since that's standard in the industry, and buy a separate book for this. Monthly statements must be compared with daily receipts and, if in good order, be paid promptly to keep up your credit standing. Liquor bills must be paid by a date each month mandated by law. Repair and maintenance bills are frequently settled on completion of the work. Credit-card forms must be submitted often for payment. Deposits of cash and checks must be made daily (this is the best part!) and bank statements checked. Prepare yourself—and set up your office —for this side of proprietorship as well.

You've no doubt heard that running a restaurant demands long hours every day. It's true. But your hours are *not* consumed, usually, in a constant round of all work and no play. While you'll have certain daily duties to attend to, a good part of your day consists of "work" that is downright delightful. Acting as maître d', greeting and seating your patrons, relaxing at your own bar with friends or lively company, enjoying your own cuisine (without a bill presented at meal's end!), interviewing, sampling new foods and wines—all these comprise a good part of those "long hours," too. Once your establishment is running along smoothly, you'll find that you'll spend a good amount of your time simply *enjoying* it.

One of the great charms of the restaurant industry is the fact that payments for goods received are made *on the spot.* No sending out of invoices (unless you allow personal credit accounts) or waiting months for a check to arrive in the mail. Settlement checks from American Express, Diner's Club, and the like are usually in your hands within a week at most, while the bank-issued credit cards (Visa, MasterCard, etc.) are credited immediately, as cash, when you make your bank deposit.

However, you must be prepared to exercise tight controls on all that beautiful incoming cash, to avoid any sticky-fingered temptations. We discuss methods of accomplishing this in a separate chapter entitled "Inventory and Guest Check Control." Even before you open, however, make arrangements with your bank for odd-hours deposits, and plan to vary the times of any bank trips you make.

To review: Plan to learn personally all aspects of your restaurant's operation from management to cooking, bartending, and waiting tables, on down to dishwashing. Attempt simple repairs yourself, and build up a file of competent mechanics for each type of emergency. Learn to keep proper books, or hire a part-time professional to do it for you. Set up a control system for cash flow and inventory supply. Make frequent bank trips.

Sound reasonable to you? Not too confining? Good. Then bound ahead. You'll make a *fine* restaurateur.

2

WHAT KIND RESTAURANT?

Restaurants run the gamut from Meals on Wheels to nightclubs in the sky. While it's a bit unlikely you'd want to go to either of those extremes, chances are you do have in mind the type of restaurant you'd like to open. At least a general idea? All the better if you do.

There are two really basic queries to which you must address yourself in this area, and if you already have a particular kind of restaurant in mind, you're half way along.

The very first question you must ask yourself is: *What kind of restaurant do I really want to open?* What's it to be? A pub? A cafeteria? A fast-food operation? A quiet dining room? A *bustling* dining room? A tearoom? A pizza parlor? An ice cream extravaganza? A supper club? A bar with sandwiches? A dining room with a service bar? A full bar? A coffee house? All of the above?

What kind of menu will you be offering? Italian? Pancake house? Oriental? All-American? Steak house? Fish specialty? French? English? Eskimo?

Once you have established *in your mind* just what it is

you'd like to provide, then you can go on to Question Two
—the really essential one, I expect. To wit: *Does the restaurant I propose to open fill a* need *in its community?*

Your answer to this question *must* be an unconditional
yes. We've chosen to ask it right here at the beginning of
this handbook because it's absolutely basic to your success. You've heard, no doubt all too often, that the restaurant business is among the riskiest in the world, that the
number of failures outweigh successes two to one or
worse, etc., etc. All true. *But*—most of these risky businesses, those failures, were all but doomed from the very
beginning because they offered their respective communities nothing, or at best very little, that those areas didn't
already enjoy.

Just because good old Charlie and Jane are doing an
overflow business with their little French restaurant
across the street does *not* mean that the avenue is wide
open for a duplicate. Even the big-name franchisers can
bite the dust when they go too far, saturating a shopping
area, for example, with three or four chains all offering
essentially the same burgers and fries.

If a restaurant in your chosen neighborhood has recently closed, try to secure a copy of its recent menu to
determine, if you can, why nobody seems to miss it. This
is especially true if that's the vacant store *you're* considering. Chances are it offered nothing unique to the neighborhood, merely copying its more successful competitors
nearby. Such "failed" establishments were, as you can
see, failures at the start, and should never have opened
at that particular location with that particular menu.

Now, don't *you* make that mistake. If you've always
wanted to open a steak house, but the area you're consid-

7

ering already has two or three good ones, *don't open your steak house in that neighborhood.* Either change your cuisine (try an Italian menu—there's a lot more profit in pasta than steak, anyway) or change communities. If you will really do this—*thoroughly* check out the area in which you intend to build your new restaurant with the thought uppermost of giving that community something it wants and needs—you will probably never be a negative statistic.

Quiz Question: What's wrong with this location?

Use your good judgment, too, in the selection of your site for projected customer turnover. *Don't* build your cozy tearoom on a fast, four-lane superhighway and expect very many to stop by. *Don't* select a predominantly residential community for a noisy drive-in—your neighborhood peers will hound you out of business in six months. Check out the local zoning regulations that may apply in any location you select *before* doing anything further. That sounds self-evident, I know, but in the flurry of real-estate details, such obvious points can easily be overlooked. Some communities, for example, may restrict the actual number of restaurants allowed within a given number of blocks. Others may restrict the serving of liquor on the premises. The only way you can be certain about these things is to check first with the department of buildings or planning commission of your chosen community. It's an ounce of prevention.

Do build a fast-food restaurant opposite a college campus, near a new set of office buildings, or in a shopping mall, if it will fill a need there. *Do* select the main street of an affluent suburb for your French, Italian, Chinese, or All-American steak house. Place a pancake house near a large, active church and school. In other words, use good, simple common sense in the selection of your site, and don't let anyone pressure you into a location until you've had the opportunity to get to really know it. After all, you'll be living a lot of your waking life there. Be sure you like it, or forget it.

Finally, a word about decor. The presentation of your restaurant—its physical appearance inside and out—often determines its character as much as your name and menu in the window. Money budgeted for decor, unless it's overdone, is rarely misspent. Often customers will be moved to try a new dining room simply because "we liked the looks of the place." This aspect of your new restaurant is, in fact, so important to your success that I've devoted a full chapter specifically to it.

Whatever it takes—good food, filling a community need, the right site, attractive decor (probably all of it)—give it to your patrons and friends. They, in turn, will give *you* prosperity, and the sense of pride that comes with creating a really popular spot.

3

THE PRIME
IMPORTANCE
OF LOCATION

I once asked a prominent fast-food chain operator what he considered the three most essential qualities of a successful restaurant. He answered immediately: "Location, location, and third, location."

Exaggerated a bit as that answer may be, it points up an all-important fact of life for the would-be entrepreneur in the restaurant field. All the good food, modest prices, fabulous decor, and friendly staff in the world are lost and useless to you if your customers can't *find* you. Have you ever spent hours riding around, especially in the country, trying to find that "marvelous little place where the steaks melt off your fork," only to wind up, tired and discouraged, at Elmer's Eats?

If the site you select is of paramount importance, it follows that this, then, is the first thing you should consider as soon as you've decided on the kind of restaurant you are going to create, and gotten your capitalization together (see Chapter 4). Once you know how much money you have at your disposal, spend all your time and effort from there on in finding a good spot. Do not expect to be crowned with success in a day or two (it sometimes takes months), and for that reason, refuse to be hurried along at this vital stage of your venture.

The perfect site for you will depend, of course, on the kind of operation you're planning. There are, however, some good general considerations that will hold true for almost every potential restaurant location. Let's take a look at some of them here:

- Try to find a location on one of the *main* roads in your area, the ones that are the most traveled in the hours you plan to be open. In general, scorn sites on side streets, even if they are only a few hundred yards away from the main thoroughfare. It's axiomatic in this business that—given the same menu, equipment, size, and staff—a restaurant on a busy street will do twice the volume as one around the corner from it.

- Keep your new restaurant on *ground level*, even in big cities. For some unknown reason, customers seem to hate to climb stairs. They can be induced to descend a few steps into a pleasant restaurant, but rare indeed is the successful dining room whose main entrance is on the second floor. Perhaps this is the reason second floors are always available, even in the most crowded communities.

- Your building or store will have to possess *at least* two full exits, preferably with one to the rear or side, or you will not be able to secure a permit to open a restaurant there. Restaurant regulations are more stringent than those that apply to the average store.

- If you are planning to open in the country, be certain that not only will the site you select be able to provide ample customer parking space, but that access roads to and from your location are possible and easy from *both* lanes of traffic.
- Corner locations are almost always best in both town and country. For one thing, both foot and automobile traffic are slowed down there. Also, any place with double exposure has twice the chance to sell itself. And entrances, access, and parking are all made easier on the corner.
- If you're renting or leasing, check out the reputation of the former tenants. In some cities you will be denied a liquor license, for example, for a number of years if the previous proprietors at the location were caught doing something shady.
- Before signing any leases or buying an old building, consult with the local landmarks association, if there is one in the community. Sometimes—if your building is in a "historic district"—you will be unable to make *any* outside structural changes whatever. What's more, you will have to appear before a local board for approval even for your outside signs, lights, and choice of paint colors!
- Do not open an English pub in and Irish neighborhood. And vice versa.
- Finally, as we mentioned in the previous chapter, check out your prospective neighborhood thoroughly to ascertain that the new restaurant you propose to create will fill some sort of *need* in that community. If there already exist two or

three thriving restaurants of the same general character as the one you are planning, move on to another site where the competition will not only be less, but where you will be welcomed unreservedly by your prospective customers.

4

FINANCING—RAISING THE TAB

Most new restaurants fail simply because insufficient money was available to pull them through. There are always *some* unforeseen expenses, *some* emergencies. A totally fixed budget is bound to crumble a bit at the edges.

To avoid this happening to you, take a good, hard look right now at all the sources of capital that you, personally, have available. Let's examine such resources together here, so you will be able to determine in advance what to expect. Making all the calculations suggested in this chapter will tell you immediately if you have enough of the green to start your own venture.

Adequate working capital can be estimated by applying your own answers to these nine essential proposals:

1) What is the *total* cost outlay, including surcharges, legal costs, and taxes, of the purchase of the land?
2) Does your property already have adequate sewerage for the operation of a restaurant? If not, it might be financial folly to proceed.

3) Have you sufficient space for parking and a separate garbage disposal area? Is adjacent space available on workable terms for any of this?

4) Are there zoning laws or other restrictions that might apply to your proposed plot? If you are planning a bar, are you sufficiently far from churches and schools to comply with the local liquor laws?

5) If you're leasing, most of the above applies, as well as:
   A. Is your rent spelled out in advance in your lease?
   B. Does your lease run for *at least* ten years?
   C. Are you hoist for any share of your landlord's increased taxes (*some* is normal)? Do you know what they are likely to amount to?

6) If you're constructing your own building, have you secured a "completed job" estimate of *all* costs?

7) Make up a comprehensive list of each of the following operating expenses. Refer to the listing at the back of the book for guidance in each of these catagories:
   A. Heavy kitchen equipment.
   B. Bar equipment (including refrigerators).
   C. Chairs, tables, booths, serving tables, ice machines.
   D. Flooring (kitchen, dining room, storage, and refuse area).
   E. Dining room decor.
   F. Inside and outside lighting.
   G. Minor equipment (pots, dishware, silver, glasses, cleaning equipment, menus, busing tables, and trays).

H. Food, beverage, and liquor "start-up" costs.
I. Installation and maintenance of heating and air conditioning.
J. Advertising, publicity, and printing.
K. Professional help (attorney, accountant, architect, designer).
L. Licensed help (electricians, plumbers, consultants, etc.).
M. Security and insurance costs.
8) Figure yearly costs for laundry and cleaning/maintenance.
9) Ask your accountant or attorney for a detailed estimate of *all* taxes and operating license fees for your entire first year.

If you have been completely honest with yourself (and why even bother otherwise?), your answers to the above points will supply you with an overall *minimum* figure you will need to get started. Now add 10 percent more to the total to cover some of your unexpected expenses. One restaurateur we knew found his basement filled up with water after every heavy rainstorm. Now, *that's* an unexpected expense!

Raising capital is almost always a personal venture. Unless you're extraordinarily persuasive, you will need to begin with a fair amount of your *own* "seed money" —preferably in cold cash or easy negotiables—as a foundation fund for your new restaurant. It's almost futile to try to raise cash without some money of your own to invest.

Relatives and friends are the most obvious first choice to approach for financial assistance in getting off the ground. Their investment will always be, basically, in *you*, of course, and in your own abilities to bring about any reasonable venture you set your mind to do. Your responsibilities to them, in turn, are even greater than normal.

Banks, generally speaking, are reluctant these days to invest in new ventures per se. And restaurants have never been one of their favorites, even in the best of times. They will often lend money, however, on such items as kitchen equipment, your air-conditioning unit, cash register, or other slow-depreciating items in your restaurant. All this means, really, is that you may be able to finance *some* payments, thus reducing the total amounts necessary to get open. Some dealers in new kitchen equipment may allow you an installment payment plan if you place most of your business with them. Ask about this *before* you make any major equipment purchases.

If you plan to incorporate, you can, of course, sell shares in your new restaurant as a capital-raising expedient. Be careful, if you do this, not to lose controlling interest yourself. Put these matters directly into the hands of your attorney.

Some government agencies have been instituted to help the smaller businessman. However, they usually all involve a good deal of waiting time, much red tape, and uncertainty. Many government bureaucrats look to the turtle as a model of speed and dexterity. Try to raise your capital in the private sector first, keeping any government assistance as a last-ditch effort if all else fails.

Naturally, if you're planning to do something *really* different—an all-American Indian menu, for instance, with only full-blooded Indians as staff—then, perhaps, even an agency such as the Bureau of Indian Affairs could arrange to help you. For government assistance of any kind, your chances are greatly improved if you can offer some employment in any disadvantaged or handicapped areas.

Franchising is another financial route, one especially recommended to those who are both young and somewhat undercapitalized. All franchise plans are different, however. Check them all out carefully, and bear in mind these points in particular:

1) Sign no contract until you and your attorney (both) thoroughly understand all the provisions.
2) Calculate ahead for a period of five years or so. Where will you be then, financially? Where do you want to be?
3) Understand completely who owns *what* in your franchise arrangements.

Remember, though—with any franchise you are *not* creating your *own* restaurant.

A final word of financial advice. If you're planning to run your new restaurant yourself, with or without working partners, you can cut your initial first year's operating costs down by the amount of the salary of one or two managers. This implies that you will not take out anything except living expenses for the first few months for yourself. Such a strategy may be crucial for the success of your first year of business, as you struggle to solicit, find, and keep a clientele who will make your restaurant a habit in their daily lives.

Traditionally, a maiden restaurant—being the new one on the block—will receive overwhelming attention during the opening few weeks. The doorway will be over-crowded. You'll be rushed off your feet—and all this, mind you, when you're least organized. Gradually, how-ever, your clientele will filter down to those who really like you, and find your place a convenient and happy watering hole. So, in contrast to your opening weeks, you'll probably experience a few empty tables after you've been open only a couple of months. By now, every-one nearby knows you are there and has heard some-thing, good or bad, about your new establishment. You are no longer headline news.

This is the critical period, when you must do every-thing in your power to build up patronage while continu-ing to please those who have already found you. Keep your standards rigorously high during this period—they will be more needed at this time than they ever will be again. Do some promoting, some advertising, a lot of "specials." Seek out small parties, and cater to them *in* your restaurant.

You will then begin to fill up a little bit more each week, as word of mouth (the best advertising in the world) starts to function in your favor. Once you've reached full capacity, then it's time to consider reservations. You've made it! You are "established."

Prepare, therefore, for the likelihood of this business phenomenon by allowing enough extra capital on hand to cover you during your first few months of operation *should it be necessary.* It is here, frankly, where many restaurants fail. And it can all be avoided if you do not spend *every* penny opening up, but allow for some reason-able reserves to keep your doors open for a bit until you find your rightful niche in the community.

After that, you'll never look back.

5

BUILD
OR BUY?

If you've already found that perfect spot on which to build your new restaurant from the ground up, you don't need a book to congratulate you. The advantages to you are many—no escalating rents, no leases to expire. You'll own your own building and can do with it anything that the laws allow. You'll be able to construct your restaurant pretty much according to your specific needs, with very little compromise. You'll be able, probably, to provide for ample parking, and for hidden refuse pickup. And your establishment can be designed and built the exact size you have in mind now, with provisions for future expansion, if desired, already rendered.

It'll take a bit o' the green, of course, up front. But so does remodeling or restructuring an already existing building. Assuming that you can handle all financing necessary, building your own restaurant physically from your own plans cannot be topped.

Next in preference is the remodeling of an already established or prebuilt restaurant that meets with your general aims. If, however, you have to pay for the present owner's years of "good will" in addition to the actual equipment, the final total needed to buy can be almost as much as building your own from scratch.

But buying a "going" restaurant—assuming it's a successful one, of course—*does* have the marvelous advantage for you of an already pretested business. You know what you can expect from the very moment of takeover. Actual income begins right away, too. If you can improve on the former owner's image or menu (or both), you'll be further ahead faster than any other way, improving your investment accordingly as you hit your stride.

Should you purchase an established business, try to buy the building as well, if you possibly can. The Italians have an age-old axiom that contends it is always best to "own your own four walls." They are dead right.

Suppose the already existing restaurant is *not* successful, however—what then? Then, *beware*. Look over all factors of location, kind of menu, management, the age of the owners, the size of the house, and the general condition of the place. Again ask yourself the prime question: Does the restaurant fit the needs or the habits of its own neighborhood?

Finally, remodeling a building or a floor or two to create a new restaurant in someone else's building will require a lease (unless you can get an option to buy the whole building by a certain date) that will allow you to make the needed renovations and, above all, provide you enough time—ten years, at a *minimum*—to recoup the costs of these renovations. This, usually, is the least expensive way actually to devise your own restaurant, and is the route most beginning entrepreneurs take. Costs will vary, depending on the amount of actual renovation you require and, of course, the labor market at the time and place you choose. Do remember, however, that all structural changes you make in a leased or rented building belong, henceforth, to the landlord.

Whichever method you find best for you, there are certain conditions you must check out *before* doing anything whatever. Some questions that will need answers are:

- Is the land, subdivision, or street zoned commercially for a restaurant? The planning department in the community will quickly tell you.
- What are the taxes? Check state, county, and local taxes to be paid. Is the community you're thinking of entering growing so fast they'll have to build additional new schools in the near future? That almost inevitably leads to higher taxes all around.
- Is there proper drainage?
- Is your chosen spot anywhere near an undesirable business (such as iron-mongering) that will give off bad fumes, noises, or vibes?
- Is there a restaurant similar to yours already established nearby? Are they packed to overflowing on nights *other* than weekends? Are they successful or just hanging on? Are they for sale?
- What are the commercial utility rates?
- Is there adequate fire and police protection?
- If already built, what insurance record does the building have?
- If your plans include a bar or liquor service at table, check the neighborhood for a school or a church within easy distance. Should you find one, measure the distance betwixt you on the town

map, then verify this fact with the state liquor authority to be sure you'll be allowed a license.

- Are there any local or county regulations on the books that would prohibit (or limit) your building or establishing a restaurant in a given location? Check this with a local attorney rather than take anyone's word for it, since confusion abounds about such ordinances.

- Is the existing building structurally sound? Roof leak? Need new wiring or plumbing? (Probably.) Basement damp? Ground firm? Talk with a building inspector and/or a land surveyor before you make a move.

- Will you be located in an historic district of any kind? If you suspect so, look into any regulations that may be required for the exterior of your building, and if permits are needed. You may even have to submit your architectural plans for approval.

- Are there any special taxes, locally, that would apply to your new restaurant? (New York City, for example, has an outrageous commercial *rent* tax!)

- Finally, are the taxes or your rent/lease terms in keeping with the average business trends in that community? Snoop around in the neighborhood a bit. Don't hesitate to call on the local chamber of commerce and spell out exactly what you propose to them. They can be valuable allies in getting you started properly—as well as future good customers.

6

ADVANCE MENU PLANNING

These days, when the only thing higher than this week's market basket is the projected price of *next* week's, how in the world does a restaurateur figure out his or her menu in advance?

There are general rules governing your everyday pricing, which will be discussed more fully in Chapter 15. At this time, however, all I want you to do is gather together a prospective menu for your new place. It's important to you for several reasons.

The type of menu you may have in mind—and most restaurateurs begin with this thought fairly well defined —should undergo a bit of examination before you can comfortably settle down with it. It's of little value, for example, to erect a sign on your new premises proclaiming "Cincinnati's Newest and Finest French Restaurant" when your budget tells you that the utmost you will be able to swing in sophisticated entrées is egg foo young. Don't overreach, in other words, especially at the start.

Ah, but you want to offer gourmet cuisine? Heaven knows the country could do with a few more places to get a gourmet meal. Well, let's see. Begin with an honest appraisal of all your available funds. Be aware that a truly fine, haute-cuisine menu will require an equally haute price for special kitchen equipment. You will require better-than-average silver, china, and glassware. And, above all, unless you're extraordinarily skilled—a true chef—and plan to do the prepping and cooking yourself, you'll need one or two highly trained chefs in your kitchen as well as a pantry assistant.

It's true, of course, that such fine cooking deserves—and gets—good prices on the menu. If you are going to put out all that effort, you are, indeed, entitled to charge healthy entrée prices. This brings us to your second self-examination question: Will the neighborhood support such a restaurant in sufficient numbers to make the enterprise profitable for you? Given truly fine cuisine, will the people of your community appreciate it, and patronize you often? Can they afford you?

If you can come up with honest affirmative answers here, then *be certain* that you provide enough in your budget to enable you to offer the best, and not have to shave any corners. The most profitable single restaurants in the world are outrageously priced, usually, with truly superb cuisine and fine wines. It takes constant vigilance and everyday attention to all details to gain and maintain such a reputation at a constantly high level. And it requires total dedication on the part of its owners and managers, year after year.

All that may be just a bit more than you can afford to bring about. After all, relatively few communities can support more than one or two gourmet establishments. Anything less requires a *lot* less risk and, certainly, a great deal less work.

Whatever menu you choose, your restaurant should

strive to incorporate some *theme*—something distinct and apart from the others—that will distinguish it, and keep it recurring in the minds of your prospective patrons when they get hungry for certain foods in particular. Ethnic menus—Chinese, Italian, German, for example—accomplish this neatly. So do menus featuring steaks, pizza, hoagies and similar specialties, seafood, and pancakes. If you can, consider the wide ranges possible here before making any final decisions on your own menu.

You should know that many food specialties, in individual or mass portions, can be purchased frozen but otherwise fully prepared for you. All you need is the oven to heat them, and a waiter or waitress to serve. Does this sound like the *other* end of the scale from haute cuisine? It sure is. And while such items can, in a pinch, be utilized as daily specials, particularly in moderately priced restaurants, during rush hours at lunch or dinnertime, in no way—and make no mistake about this—should you depend on them, since they will prove to be considerably more costly to use on a per-portion average. And, frankly, while sometimes tasty, most frozen commercial entrées possess a bland taste requiring seasoning and a bit of "beefing up" before serving. For that amount of effort, you can usually produce the entrée yourself.

Already prepared frozen desserts, however, are frequently splendid. Try some. They would be a very much simpler solution for you than attempting to make desserts—especially in a wide variety—on your own premises unless you enjoy baking. They will also keep perfectly until needed.

The least expensive entrées to offer, from the standpoint of the initial cost of the ingredients, are pizza, most

Chinese dishes, pancakes, and the many varieties of pastas and sauces. Both French and Italian cooking frequently utilize the less expensive cuts of meats in many of their dishes—it's the preparation, the herbs, and the lovely sauces that make them so delicious.

In a chapter as necessarily general as this one, all we are attempting to accomplish here is to point out some menu possibilities to you, together with some advice on just what it will take to bring your own particular menu into reality. But you, personally, *must* settle on your choice of cuisine and the approximate number of dishes you plan to offer *before* you can effectively plan your kitchen area and secure the proper equipment for it.

The time has come to begin thinking of specifics for your new restaurant. Once you have snagged the right place in the right location, your menu becomes the most important decision you must make. Write it out *now*. Chapter 15 will help you in pricing and quality control, as well as suggest some extremely practical menu entrées. But your own menu is always a very personal thing —the basic ingredient, after all, of your new reputation as a restaurateur. Take all the time you need here. Look at a number of menus from other successful restaurants. Perhaps—just perhaps—you may cull from some of them an idea, or a presentation or two, that may enhance your own.

One infallible guide—your own menu should make you hungry just thinking about it!

7

HOW TO
BUILD AND
SET UP A BAR

For sheer entertainment—always full to the brim with surprises—you can't beat bartending, at least for part of the time. Unless you're extraordinarily shy, you're certain to enjoy it, and, of course, it puts you in close personal touch with a fair number of your patrons. I know of no aspect of running your own restaurant that is so exciting.

Consider the mystique that has grown up about bartenders—the air of wordly-wisdom, the spirit of independence—the very soul of the top honcho. Except, perhaps, in the huge, impersonal hotels and their restaurants, have you ever met a bartender who did not possess (or so it seemed) those attributes?

The reason for this is simple. The bartender's world *is* a self-sufficient one. As a bartender you *are* in total control of your domain, completely independent of the maître d', the cooks, and busboys. While you do take orders from the waiters and waitresses, *they* are the ones who wait patiently at the side of the bar until you serve them. And, in most cases, the bartender receives at least

10 percent of the tips of those waiters and waitresses, while you share yours with no one.

Everything the bartender needs to function with such apparent ease and competence is right at hand. Since you rarely have to leave this domain—never scurry anywhere —you can keep your cool when all around you are hustling. And so the mystique begins—it's built into the job!

Of course, like so much in life, your apparent ease as a bartender is based on tight planning, placement of equipment, and easy access to all the ingredients you require. Here's what they are, but a word of caution is in order before we begin: Whatever your budget, *don't stint* in this area of your planning. The bar, above all, *must* function smoothly—in all probability it will be responsible for a very high percentage of your profits.

You will need:

The bar itself
Stools, one for every three feet if loose
A back bar, preferably with lowboy refrigerators
A cash register
At least one three-position sink, with drainboards on
    both ends of it
A draft beer dispenser system
A speed rack
Wine racks
At least one open ice bin
A seltzer dispenser, and tank storage space
Glassware and shakers
A used bottle and trash area
Skidproof slats on the flooring behind the bar
An ice-making machine

Abundant shelving for liquor bottle display and for
   reserves
Extra refrigerators (optional)
Cutting boards
Shelving for glassware and beer mugs
Miscellaneous ashtrays, coasters, stirrers, etc.
A telephone at hand

Let's look at each of these requirements for building
your bar, bearing in mind that as a proprietor or builder
you must adapt each of these suggestions into the space
you have available. Your floor plan, then, is the first step.
Check it out thoroughly, and try to place your water
pipes, drains, and even the electrical panel in the bar
area for easy access. Place the bar as much as possible
directly over a basement area that can be utilized for a
cold or walk-in box, to accommodate your draft beer lines.
Make certain that you allot an area big enough to include
the back bar with refrigerators, the bar itself, stool placement, and some standing room. If in doubt, however, allot
the bar area *more* rather than lesser space (unless you
are only setting up a service bar, and expect to serve no
one at it) because it will prove to be the single, most
popular spot of all in your restaurant. Not only will you
hope to build up a nice, neighborhood bar clientele, but
this is invariably the spot most people choose to wait for
tables to become available when you're busy. As such, the
bar area must *never* be cramped in its design.

THE BAR ITSELF

There is really no great mystery about a good bar, and
you or your contractor can build one from scratch into the
restaurant if you so choose. But first secure an estimate

from your carpenter, and then investigate the cost of a new or used professionally built one in your area. Usually these are not only the best, in workmanship and materials, but the least expensive in the long haul. Use the Yellow Pages, and check out both Bar Suppliers and Restaurant Suppliers, New and Used.

Best of all, of course, is a bar already in the building, which you can proceed to adapt. Next best, usually, is a used bar. They can be cut down or, with the aid of a good carpenter, lengthened. A truly fine old-fashioned bar has an indelible patina and a classic style that is all but impossible to duplicate. If one of these fits your decor, check out the auction or bankruptcy sales notices in your local newspaper (or in those of the nearest large city) for restaurants with full bars that are on the block. Frequently, by the way, back bars, stools, refrigerators, and such are also available from the same source. Check with your local liquor and beer salesmen (they will find *you* the minute you begin, never fear!) and anyone in your area dealing with used restaurant equipment.

Don't forget the brass foot railing. If it isn't provided with your bar, you can purchase a new or used one from the same sources and adapt it. But you *gotta* have one, not only for an authentic appearance, but for practical reasons, too—without one, your nice new bar will be kicked in, literally, in a few short months.

BAR STOOLS

These are built in a truly fascinating variety of sizes and styles, and it's fun trying them all out before deciding which to supply your place. Used stools are usually not worth the bother, unless they have been installed only a short time. New ones are available at wholesale prices at restaurant equipment stores, and the larger the store the better. Try not to rely on catalogs when purchasing—select a style you can personally try out in the shop if at all possible. The bar stool is far more important than many realize, if for no other reason than its comfort (or lack of it) will ultimately have a good deal to do with the success of the bar itself. Allow at least three feet of space for each stool, more if you can, if it's to be a swivel type. Avoid built-in stationary stools, since your bar patrons will appreciate some mobility, particularly during a prolonged stay.

Upholstered or not is a matter for your own decision. But on no account settle for a cheaply built set—you'll only be back a year later, a bit wiser, to reorder. And remember—these bar stools take a terrific beating. Not only are they constantly in use, but they are, after all, rarely handled with care. Whatever style you ultimately choose, make 'em *staunch*.

BACK BAR

Here we have the single most important piece of equipment in your entire bar setup. First of all, the back bar is what your customers will be looking at for a good portion of the time and, as such, sets the mood and tone for the entire restaurant. Exercise your creativity in this area as much as possible, and don't be afraid of a "busy" appearance—nothing is worse than a dreary, tidy bar. Your liquor and beer salespeople will supply you with a good quantity of advertising material, some of which (certainly not all!) will look very good if properly used and in keeping with your overall decor. Don't be afraid to use it, and to change it frequently.

The back bar, of course, serves as the prime functioning

area for the bartender. It will contain, usually, one or two refrigerators in the lower portion, shelving for your liquor displays, a cash register, probably glassware storage, and—most important—a flat surface used for prepping, slicing, guest-check totaling, and kindred other uses. It is, really, the "office" of the restaurant itself.

A proper back bar, then, is of prime importance, and

A typical back bar.

should be as commodious as you can afford to make it. Never build in one that is less than three feet in depth. Again, you can adapt a used one (but rework the refrigerators) or, probably best in most circumstances, build one in yourself, blending both new and old pieces into a unit. This could also be your most inexpensive method— and, if properly done, can result in a spectacular back bar.

Most back bars feature mirrors, but be careful to either mute this area with your liquor bottle display, use toned or "antiqued" glass mirrors, or limit the square footage to the extent that your patrons are not forced to look at themselves every time they face forward.

Always build in a fair amount of open, flat working surface. It will fill up astoundingly fast.

Refrigerators in the base portion of your back bar will prove not only to be convenient, but they are traditional, and your bartender will expect them there. You can situate them under the bar itself, of course, or any other place, but the depth of your back bar makes for a nicely sized reach-in box, usually with two shelves, for at-hand cold storage of bottled beer, white and rosé wines, and your citrus fruits. And since it's easy to get at, it's easy to keep clean and dry.

I feel it's extremely important to ask your electrician to attach your bar refrigerators to a separate set of compressors, assuming your units are not self-contained, so that the bar and the kitchen have emergency refrigerators to utilize if needed. This sounds self-evident, and it is, but it is incredible how many restaurants have ignored this rule. Malfunctioning of compressors is one of the recurring problems in all restaurants. It follows that the fewer refrigerators or freezers you hook up together, the less the strain on any of the compressors.

CASH REGISTER

Your bar will require one of these even if you do not plan to take in cash there. All beverages that stem from the bar—and that includes orange juice and Shirley Temples—need to be rung up before you serve them. Without one, you will abdicate all your controls.

Registers vary from the simple, old-fashioned windups with beautiful brass fretwork (to be used for display *only*) to highly sophisticated numbered and keyed machines. Here, too, I'd advise you to secure the very best you can afford, since honesty frequently becomes a virtue when it's enforced. The more safeguards you build in, the harder it will be (but never impossible, sorry to say) for a bartender to exercise a light touch.

Since cash registers are, unfortunately, never cheap, you might check out these, too, at auctions. Your local office machine suppliers will have a selection of used and reconditioned machines as well. Registers have been extraordinarily sophisticated for some years now, so a machine half a dozen years old or less should prove quite adequate if your budget is tight. If not, simply buy a new one. It's the backbone of your business.

THREE-POSITION SINKS

Before buying *any* sinks for your bar, check first with your Health Department for their requirements and sizes. Most will have a booklet or a brochure for you. This alone will save you many headaches, since bar sinks are individually fitted and built in, and woe to the proprietor who builds in one that proves to be too small. Some localities may also require an electric glass washer behind the bar. You'll find that out on the same visit to the Health Department.

By all means provide for plenty of drainboard space on *both* sides of the sinks. Design what you think would be about right, and then almost *double* the width! When bartenders are busy, they cannot take the time to wash dirty glasses, but they have to get them off the bar and stow them *somewhere* until they can get to them. Guess where? Uh-huh, on the drainboards. Keep your bartender (and you) happy—make the drainboards very wide indeed.

DRAFT BEER DISPENSERS

At this writing, your various beer distributors will still supply you with *some* of the equipment you'll need to serve draft beer. They should be able, too, to put you on to a proper plumber who is trained to do this specialized job correctly. He, in turn, can teach you how to properly maintain and clean the machines so you'll be able to take care of some of the future maintenance yourself.

The draft beer itself comes in one-half and full barrel sizes, the former being the easiest, naturally, to handle and the most popular. Essential to serving draft beer, however, is some sort of a cold storage room, preferably below stairs, where your barrels can be stored and hooked up but kept at the correct temperature at all times. Except in Europe, this implies refrigeration. A walk-in room, at least eight to ten feet square, is by far the best, since it can be utilized as well for storage of meats and produce that require cold but not freezing temperatures.

Your contractor can build you one of these—but be sure it's insulated!—or they can be purchased in prefab form and set up.

Behind the bar, however, you'll need the beer dispensers built in, and a small drain sink to catch any draft overflow. Set this up near your bar sinks, and you can utilize the same drains. Check with your beer distributors first to determine which, if any, will provide some of this equipment on loan to you. At the very least, they'll provide those delightful pull handles—with their own advertising on 'em, naturally.

SPEED RACK

This is a simple, narrow rack that holds about a dozen or so of the most called-for brands of the most popular liquors. It is affixed, usually, just below the bar surface, out of sight but within easy—and frequent—reach of the bartender. At least one, more if you have the space, is a must. They are not expensive and, considering the constant use they receive, surprisingly hardy.

WINE RACKS

Not only do they look great behind a bar, but, if placed on high, provide an easy system for keeping wine horizontal yet accessible. You'll sell more bottles of wine, too, if you feature racks. Always keep them full, and provide space in them for half bottles, as well.

OPEN ICE BINS

Even if you can afford the space for an ice machine under the bar, you'll need an open-topped ice bin—at least one—for at-hand use. Almost all drinks these days

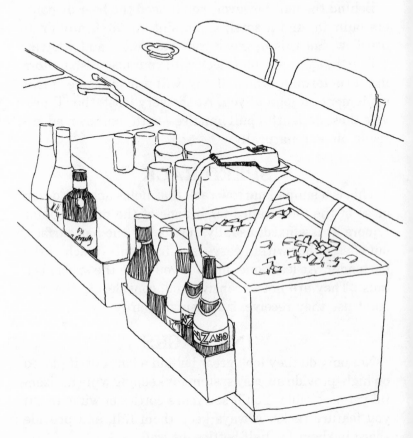

A typical speed rack.

require ice, and the busy bartender needs a handy open bin to scoop ice with a glass or shaker. It should be placed as close as possible to the most needed glasses and the seltzer dispenser.

THE SELTZER "SNAKE"

Indispensable to making the average bar concoction is
a cobra-headed seltzer dispenser known to saloon cogno-

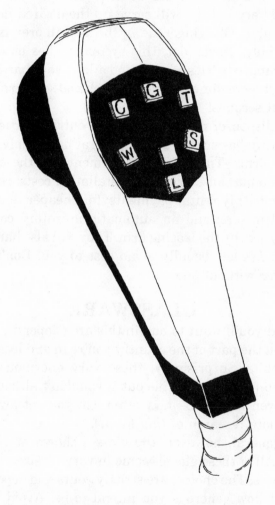

A "seltzer snake" dispenser.

CREATING A SUCCESSFUL RESTAURANT

scenti as "the snake." Connected to a seltzer machine and several tanks of syrup in the basement or under the bar, the dispenser does, indeed, resemble a snake in that its six-sided head contains several buttons that, when pushed very lightly, will serve up the desired mix, be it tonic water, cola, ginger ale, or the like, all premixed with the bubbly. Never flat, this system makes obsolete all those capped bottles of soda, and allows your bartender to mix and serve, for example, a scotch and soda in about six to eight seconds!

The dispenser may be purchased outright or leased on a monthly basis from any of several bar supply or soda supply firms. The lease arrangement has these advantages: no purchase price; no installation costs; relatively small monthly rental payments; far cheaper to use than bottled mixers; and an automatic inventory control of your syrups by the leasing firm. They will also handle any repairs needed, usually at no cost to you. Don't set up your bar without one.

GLASSWARE

What you'll want to buy in this area depends, in large part, on the part of the country you're in and local drinking habits. Surprisingly, these vary enormously from place to place. Check this out if you don't already know (and even if you do—how often can you get away with legitimate research of *this* kind?).

In general, however, the glasses shown at right are basic. All of these glasses come in varying sizes, differing by ounces. The choices are strictly yours and depend a lot on just how generous you intend to be. Avoid oversize glassware, however—not only will you regret it, but they

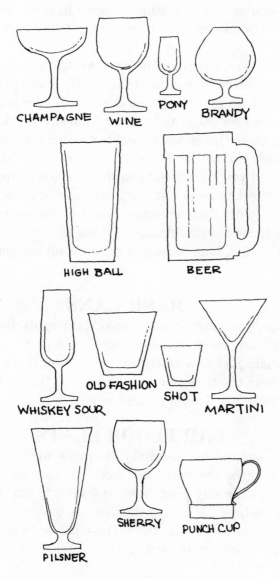

Essential glassware.

cost twice as much, a point to keep in mind when you consider breakage. This is especially true of the brandy snifter.

For an average restaurant and bar, seating from eighty to one hundred, buy at least four to six dozen of each for starters, with an extra three dozen of the basic highball glass, the beer mug, and the medium-sized cocktail and wine glasses. Unless you expect to produce a special drink for which you will be known, don't get fancy, at least at first, until you know what your breakage will amount to. Don't forget to secure at least two sizes of glass cocktail shakers (with their chromed metal counterparts), with two to three backup glasses of these in reserve. They're essential and, hopefully, will get a grand workout every day.

TRASH CANS

Large, open-topped trash cans, preferably lined with plastic bags, are *de rigueur* under the bar. You may not appreciate *just* how essential they are until the day you don't have the time to empty them, and they are all full to overflowing. Two is a minimum.

BAR FLOOR SLATS

Not essential but certainly desirable, for two reasons. One, it keeps the bartender from slipping on the floor, which, as the day progresses, is bound to sustain some spills. And, two, it makes the average bartender at least three inches taller than the average patron, a psychological advantage not to be underestimated!

SHELVING

An attractive display of liquor bottles on the back bar will not only mute the mirrors, if you have them, but provide some inspiration to those who don't really know *what* they'd like to drink. It informs your new bar patron what brands of his or her favorite booze you stock (always place brandies with brandies, scotches with scotches, etc.), and, of course, it looks just great to see all those brands of so many liquors within reach.

On the practical side, build your shelving on the step principle, so that each bottle can be reached readily and easily. Utilize any extra shelving space below bar level for storage of reserves of the popular brands or house whiskeys, with which to restock your speed rack as needed.

If space is at a premium, consider building a solid shelf high over the bar itself, where you can store (and display) those liquors least needed. Should you do this, be absolutely certain that you provide for a barrier to prevent bottles from tipping over. Liquor bottles landing on the heads of your customers is *not* what they meant when they asked you for a jolt.

REFRIGERATORS

You cannot really have too many of these, and depending on the volume of beer and wine you sell, you'll need at least two. They can be set either into the front or the back bar, but be sure you allow enough room for the wide lowboy refrigerator doors to swing fully open and still allow passing space. Since the doors are opened so often in the course of a day, condensation is sure to form into water at the base of the lower shelf. To avoid any buildup, figure on sponging each one out every day. You can take inventory at the same time. As we mentioned before, try to set each refrigerator up on a separate compressor, so you'll never be reduced to cooling your beer in the ice bin!

CUTTING BOARDS

Keep at least two at the ready, with several sharp knives. The bartender, it seems, is forever wedging oranges, or slicing lemons, and you cannot really use any other surface for this job.

ICE-MAKING MACHINE

You'll need one of these to supply your open ice chest under the bar, as well as for general use in the dining room. Fortunately, this machine can be installed along a wide hallway, or in some vacant corner *anywhere* (including the basement or an enclosed back-porch area) that will accommodate its fairly bulky size.

This is a piece of equipment that I advise you to rent, if at all possible. They are temperamental machines, usually, given to frequent clogging; consequently, they require a fair bit of maintenance—but after all, this machine is never turned off except by itself. All that maintenance and repair comes *free* with a rental contract, and in most localities is available even on weekends, when you most need it.

Sizes will vary, according to your needs. But all of them will produce crushed ice and ice cubes of convenient size for you day and night.

GLASSWARE SHELVING

Build a shelf or two near the waiter stand especially for glassware, and another, if possible, at the other end. Waiter stands—reserved spots at the bar for the exclusive use of the waiters or waitresses—are either at the far ends of your bar, or dead in the center, the former being the most private and least obtrusive arrangement. Glasses must be handy at this spot for everyone to use. You'll soon know which glasses are most in demand.

If space is short, once again try utilizing a shelf arrangement above the bar itself, stacking there the glasses you need least. Beer mugs, with handles, can be hung from the underside of such a shelf from small hooks, and look very publike in the bargain.

The whole ceiling may, indeed, be utilized, using parallel slats to hold stemware upside down, or more hooks for the mugs. Properly done, and not *too* high up, the effect can be spectacular.

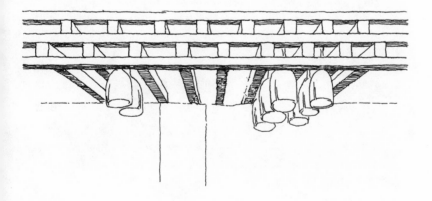

Hanging stemware.

MISCELLANEOUS EQUIPMENT

This includes those "tremendous trifles" such as ash-trays (use many), stirrers (by the carton), olives, onions, and red cherries (by the quart), and a covered dish to put them in. Coasters, bar rags, swizzle spoons, bar napkins, matches, pads of paper, and pencils are all necessary to your smooth operation. And each should always be flourished with a *smile*. Without this last item on our list, my friend, cancel all the rest, forget the restaurant business, and go in for tax collecting.

TELEPHONE

Your bar is complete when you install this infernal instrument. It must be at hand for inquiries, for ordering, and for outrageous lies about who is and who isn't sitting at your bar.

Bottoms up! Your bar is ready, now, to be stocked with all that good stuff.

8

EQUIPMENT– THE HEAVY STUFF

In this chapter I will list all the major equipment you'll need for your new restaurant. Keep a pencil handy, and write in the margins if you feel like it.

To make it simpler to understand just what you'll require, I've divided the areas to be discussed into:

> Kitchen
> Dishwashing area
> Storage
> Plumbing, heating, and wiring
> Garbage disposal
> Auxiliary rooms
> Dining room

Naturally, what *you'll* need for your own restaurant will vary somewhat from those items in the discussion that follows. But it will be the rare establishment that will not require just about every piece of *major* equipment listed here.

Use it as a guide when you go to buy (so you don't

forget, say, the toasters in all your flurry of major purchases) but add or subtract as your needs require. Remember, too, that once you've secured all this equipment, you're really ready to go! All you'll need to open your doors will be food and utensils, and a bit of patience to get your act together.

In this chapter, then, we are going to show you how to turn that empty store or hollow building into a going restaurant. *Your* restaurant. Are you excited? That dream is *really* about to come true.

KITCHEN

Let's take a look together at the major kitchen equipment you'll want, with some words of wisdom on each. Before beginning, bear in mind that virtually all these pieces come in sizes that vary from peewee to enormous, but neither of these extremes is generally desirable unless your contemplated organization will fit one of those descriptions.

As a beginning entrepreneur, you'll need to consider the following equipment for your kitchen as a minimum guide. This list is a general one, however, covering the average mid-size operation. If you're planning a pizza palace, or intend to feature baked-on-the-premises desserts, for example, you'll want to add accordingly.

    1 stove (with baking oven)
    1 to 2 broilers
    1 to 2 grills
    1 deep-fryer
    1 grill-area hood, with a large wall fan and vent
    1 fan duct to the outside

1 preparation sink
1 sandwich board
1 to 2 freezers
1 to 2 full-size refrigerators
1 to 2 lowboy refrigerators
2 toasters
1 steam table
Endless shelving
1 pass-through/over counter
1 fire protection system over the cooking area
1 knife holder
1 slicing machine
1 microwave oven
1 electric mixer (optional)
1 bun warmer (optional)
3 to 4 fire extinguishers
1 to 2 garbage holders

Costs for any of this kitchen equipment naturally vary considerably, depending on the quality, configuration, and age if previously used. However, to give you some clue to prices, I have included at the back of this book a duplicate of the list above, together with an approximate price range for *new* equipment for an eighty- to one-hundred-seat restaurant. Use it as a guide for any of this equipment you must buy. Bear in mind, too, that used and reconditioned equipment, when available, is usually priced about 40 to 50 percent *lower* than the costs quoted.

The Almighty Stove

It's the heartbeat of your kitchen, so treat it with all the care and importance it deserves. Always buy a heavy-duty institutional stove, never a home model. Your stove will be going day and night, hardly ever resting. No home unit is manufactured for that kind of use.

Six jets are a minimum, no matter how small a place you are planning to open. You will always need *at least* six jets. Don't stint on this.

Stoves come in a happy array of models for you to choose from. For example, they can be bought with an attached griddle, with or without a broiler (either below the griddle or, as a somewhat separate unit, at eye level), and with one or two baking ovens. Take your time in selection, and talk it over with your chef, if you can, to get his or her ideas on your requirements. In general, it would be far better for you to project a size too large for your immediate needs. Then when popular success comes, and you want to diversify a bit with your menus, you'll be equipped to do it.

A used cast-iron or heavy-duty stove is usually available, since they are extraordinarily hardy—indeed, they are impossible to wear out, except by neglect. Look into this possibility if your budget is a tad tight.

Broiler

As America has become more weight-conscious over the last few years, the broiler has assumed a major role in all our cooking. Even hamburgers taste better (and are better for you) if they can be broiled, at least partially. So check over your projected menu right here to determine just what role your broiler will be asked to play. If it's your thought to offer a bit of char-broiling, for example, this is best accomplished on an open-topped, open-flame unit on which you can also sear the meat. It will be devilishly smoky, however, so be sure you have the ducting and venting to carry away that residue. Filters reduce some, but not all. If your restaurant is in a noncommercial neighborhood, think twice about offering char-broiling, by the way. Nothing is worse for your public relations than to have your vented greasy smoke settling down into the backyards and open windows of your closest neighbors. It's incredible how many restaurateurs forget this when planning their menus.

Broilers can be incorporated into the stove itself, of course, and they are often built that way. But by their very design, stove broilers are somewhat inconvenient for everyday use unless your broiling needs will be extremely simple.

Far more satisfactory, usually, are one or two overhead broilers (which are not over your head at all), allowing the cook easy access. Being at eye level, he or she can see just how the meats are coming along without any stooping or, worse, guessing. For the average restaurant this is by far the best buy.

Grill and/or Griddles

These come either gas fired or electrically heated, in all sizes.

In most areas, gas is cheaper to use—no small consideration these days. If your broiling needs are simple, the easy incorporation of a broiler beneath the grill will utilize the same flames.

The chief advantage of an electric grill is the consistency of the spread of the heat over the cooking-top area. Thermostats can be set for different temperatures at one end of your griddle from the other, and they can be easily controlled. You won't need this for hamburgers, for instance, but it's highly desirable for eggs or pancakes.

Since the highest cost of your electricity will be your use of heat-inducing appliances (over 1,000 watts at least), you might take this factor into account before deciding. Check first with your local electric company to determine if they can offer you a commercial rate. If so, this may make the cost differential very little.

Gas griddles are relatively simple, and can easily be picked up in good used condition. I don't recommend you do this with an electrical appliance, however, unless you know for certain that the elements and thermostats have been replaced.

Deep-Fryers

If you're planning to serve any deep-fried foods—breaded shrimp, fishwiches, or the ubiquitous French-fried potatoes—you will need to install a deep-fryer. They are also available in both gas and electric models, and both are smoky, easily clogged, and a mess to clean out. But it's the rare restaurant that can do without one.

Whatever model you choose, get one *large* enough to cover your needs when you anticipate doing top-capacity business; dinners can be ruined while standing by, waiting for an undersized deep-fryer to handle its share. Check with a local fast-food chain to see what equipment they have installed; they have to know, since they'd be out of business without deep-fryers, wouldn't they?

In the main, unless you know it has had a very limited life to date, it's best to buy a new model. Deep-fryers are not overly expensive, and of all your major equipment, fryers lead the most violent life, succumbing to a relatively early death within a few years.

One of the secrets of a longer life for your deep-fryer, however, is simply to clean it thoroughly each time you have to change the cooking oil. (You'll know when that is, since old oil tends to turn a peculiarly nasty shade of brown. Don't wait for this to happen.) As with all your equipment, a few minutes of proper care will replace hours of trouble. Plan a specific time of day—midafternoon, say—to turn off the deep-fryer, let it cool, and clean it.

Hood, Exhaust Fan, and Vents

Sounds like a law firm, and in a way they will work like one. Each has a specific function, but they all work together toward a common end. That end is to get rid of smoke and grease.

Over your stove, grill, broiler, and deep-fryer you will need to erect a metal hood covering over the outer reaches of that equipment. Into it you will build a large exhaust fan, and it in turn will be vented, through filters (removable for easy cleaning), up the outside of your restaurant. None of this is as awesome as it sounds, thank heaven.

You will need to call in a sheet-metal firm (finding a sheet-metal firm in a small community is usually your only headache here) to measure, check your walls inside and out, and give you an estimate.

You or your contractor might also check out the local building codes as they apply to commercial businesses to be sure you comply with the regulations. Check height of hood from the tops of your equipment; size of hood required; material; and permissible paint. With regard to the exhaust fan, ascertain if there are any special filter-types recommended for it; the size it must be; and its venting capacity (these last two requirements are really one and the same). As for your venting, here again double-check capacity, height required to rise on the outside, and the distance it must be mounted from the side of your building. Do all this first. Do *not* rely upon the sheet-metal people to do it for you, since you, not they, are responsible here.

If for some reason you cannot do any of this, overcompensate in sizes. Buy a large fan with as many speeds as possible and regulate that way.

For all the brute size of the metal hood and exhaust system, it should not be a horrendous expense even made to order, as it probably will have to be. If you can, get estimates from at least three firms. If you use the checklist mentioned above, and check the building codes, you can feel free to take the lowest estimate in this instance.

Prep Sink

A preparation sink will prove to be not only uncommonly useful in your kitchen, it is—usually—a health code requirement. It need not be particularly large, and it can be fitted into an odd space. Naturally, the closer it is to any other plumbing, the simpler and cheaper it will be to install.

Sandwich Board

The most useful of the sandwich boards not only contain the usual individual stainless-steel trays for your sandwich fillings but, placed above a lowboy refrigerator, keep your food from outside temperature spoilage.

A hood usually swings over the rear portion, covering all the individual trays, while the very front is given over

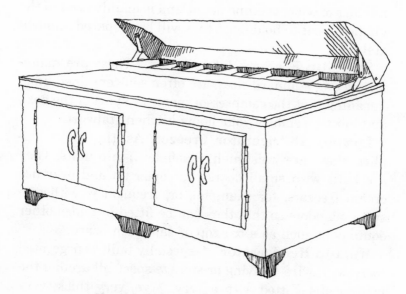

Hooded sandwich board atop a lowboy.

to a cutting board large enough to use in preparing your sandwiches. You must have one. It is one of the most versatile pieces of kitchen equipment and will seldom be left alone or unattended.

Freezers and Refrigerators

Refrigerators and freezers are different from your home models in that they are often larger, deeper, almost always of stainless steel, and sport a heftier handle. To make it easier to understand, let's divide all restaurant freezers and refrigerators into five categories, since each will have a different and separate function:

Reach-In Refrigerator/Freezer. A very *deep*, standing box, usually equipped with a remote compressor and almost always six to seven feet tall. It comes with any number of wide, opening doors, and is mainly used in the kitchen itself to hold foods that will be prepared immediately.

Stand-Up Freezer/Refrigerator. These are manufactured in standard sizes, are often self-contained units (meaning that the compressor motor is a part of the box), and most resembles your home kitchen stalwart.

Lowboy Refrigerator/Freezer. As the name implies, these are waist-high, reach-down-into units. They are built with small doors that open up and over (ice cream freezers, for example), or, frequently, with out-swinging doors so that they can be fitted in *under* other equipment such as a bar top or sandwich board.

Walk-In Refrigerator. A specially built refrigerated *room* with wire shelving or storage space all around the inner walls. Fitted with a very large, very thick, very heavy door, and slatted flooring, the room is big enough for a person to walk inside. It is invaluable to your smooth operation.

Walk-In Freezer. Exactly the same as the walk-in refrigerator, but a lot colder. Wear your ear muffs. Generally speaking, this is *not* a requirement for the average restaurant.

Since freezers and refrigerators are absolutely essential, it follows that the further your restaurant is from your source of food supplies, the more units (or larger ones) you'll require. If you have daily deliveries, your food-holding needs are proportionately less. Check this out with the dealers and wholesalers who service your town. Sometimes a wholesale dealer will help you by supplying some of your refrigeration needs. Ice cream firms often do this, as do some milk distributors. Ask them; at the same time paint a glorious picture for them regarding the enormous volume you'll be needing for your new venture as soon as you open your doors.

In any event, you will need one freezer and one refrigerator (full size) in your kitchen *at least,* and preferably side by side. You'll need others in your storage areas—fit in as many as you comfortably can, so you have some alternatives in case of an emergency.

A word here about the electric motors that drive your freezers, refrigerators, and lowboys. The power unit in each is the compressor. This is a medium-sized motor featuring a large fan belt rather like those in a small car. So that you can have the maximum space inside your appliance itself, these compressors are often "remotely" located, frequently in the basement or other storage areas. They're connected by wires and tubing, and often one such remote compressor can supply the power for more than one refrigerator/freezer box—reducing both the number of motors you'll need and the cost of running them. Check with your electrician about this.

Others are known as "self-contained," such as your home appliances are. Here the compressor motor takes up some space in the appliance itself, allowing you less capacity per unit, but without all that wiring and tubing extending off into the nether regions.

Which is best? Both, actually. On the one hand, one remote compressor can frequently handle two lowboys or a small refrigerator, so it's cheaper to run them. Since these motors are utilized day and night (although not continuously) that's no small consideration these days. With a self-contained unit, however, you will never have the worry that any *but* that unit will ever fail to function at a given time. Put another way, if a remote compressor with two refrigerators attached to it overheats and stops running, you are faced with the loss of two refrigerators at once. Where do you put their precious contents until the motor can be fixed?

So—try to even out the number of your remote vs. self-contained units so you can double up in any emergency, but still save something on your electric costs.

Check out the auctions and used-equipment dealers here. Particularly for your storage units, the refurbished refrigerator or freezer will be quite satisfactory, and about a third of the cost of a new one.

Toasters

Like everything else so far, toasters come in simple to grandiose sizes. What you'll need depends mostly on your menu. Generally speaking, one or two toasters, of institutional quality, will suffice. If you feel you'll need a lot of toast, there are marvelous machines, resembling waterfalls, that slide the bread slices up one side and down the other of an elevated treadmill; these will absolutely fascinate your customers if you can place them where they can watch them in action. All work extremely well under heavy use.

Never, never try to use a home toaster. It will last about three weeks, with luck, and can never be repaired except at the manufacturer's home office in the Arctic Circle.

Steam Table

A steam table is a waist-high piece of electric kitchen equipment not unlike the sandwich board, basically, except that it contains several fitted deep pots, with covers, for holding cooked food and retains a constant temperature for immediate serving. Cooked vegetables, gravies, sauces, pie fillings, and the like are perfect candidates for the steam table, although you or your cook will find many other ingenious ways to utilize it, too.

Often referred to as a "bain-marie," this lovely piece of equipment can also be fitted with refrigerator coils, to keep foods chilled. In either case, shelving or a small lowboy refrigerator can be built into the space below.

Shelving

Shelving hardly needs explanation, does it? You wouldn't be contemplating opening a restaurant without a pretty thorough understanding of just how important this can be. Put them up everywhere in your entire kitchen area, and design and purchase them *wide* enough to accommodate your largest pots, pans, and salad bowls. Stainless steel is best (but slippery, so incline the shelves a little bit) because it can be kept clean so easily. Failing that, paint your shelves with a glossy enamel, using several coats. Never cover them in oilcloth or self-stick paper —they're an open Homecoming invitation for roaches and all their relatives.

Pass-Through/Over Counter

Once prepared and ready to serve, the meal must reach the diner at top speed. The cooling-off process begins the instant your nice, hot entrée meets the platter. Warm the dishes, therefore, if you have the space. And be certain, as you design the pickup area, that all drafts are eliminated, or you'll have to redesign it all over again. You'd be surprised how often this simple fact is overlooked in the early layout stages. Check your blueprints *now*.

In all events, design a pass-through or pickup counter that will enable the server to get the completed order in front of your customer with minimum delay. Of course, since some waiting period is inevitable, install hot lamps overhead, and keep a reserve supply of these lamps on hand.

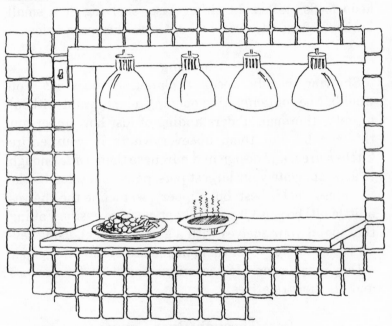

A pass-through counter with hot lamps.

In most instances, the most efficient plan will prove to be the pass-through counter, as illustrated above. It eliminates the need for your servers to trot into the kitchen area itself each time an order is ready. However, as best you can, build your pass-through counter as much *out* of the line of sight of your dining room as possible. Aesthetically, a kitchen at full tilt is rarely a thing of beauty, so spare your patrons that view. And, practically nothing is more irritating to your hungry customers than seeing a platter waiting to be picked up—they think, naturally, that it *must* be theirs and theirs alone—while the server is occupied at another table.

If it appears that a pass-through counter will not be convenient in your planning, or not in keeping with the mood and decor you project, a kitchen pickup counter will be required. Leading into it, double swinging doors with small (obligatory) windows in them are heartily advised, conspicuously labeled In and Out. (With a single swinging door, prepare to get used to the sounds of tinkling glassware and crockery.)

The pickup counter can be as basically simple as the pass-through one, or it can be designed as a self-serving area combining hot- and cold-temperature retaining trays in a bain-marie arrangement. In the latter, your waiters and waitresses will be responsible for garnishing the platters or, possibly, dishing up vegetables and such from filled receptacles at hand.

Whether in the kitchen or in the restaurant itself, a salad bar is always at hand, kept filled by the kitchen staff, for use by the waiters. Given the space, a well-stocked salad bar in the restaurant's main room for use by the patrons themselves is a lovely time-saver, and your customers will appreciate it, thinking they're getting something extra for nothing. (They are, in a way, but it's not much, really.) In either instance, allow enough space to stack salad bowls and extra silver.

A word or two here about preparation areas, which you will have to consider along with your equipment pieces as far as basic space is concerned. Build into your kitchen as many flat-surfaced areas as you can. All foods have to be cut, sliced, skinned, kneaded, diced, shredded, carved, shelled, or basted *somewhere* before hitting the stove. Woe to the cooks who find too little preparation space— they will be forced to improvise, or use shortcuts. Neither solution will work very well, of course, and tempers will rise accordingly.

A table or two—and they are built now with special hard-plastic "carving" surfaces—will be inordinately useful if you can fit them in. Failing that, the tops of your lowboy refrigerators can be adapted to made-to-order carving board tops; indeed, they can be ordered and made up for you that way.

Fire Protection System (Cooking Area)

A built-in automatic fire extinguisher system unit installed over your actual cooking area will probably be a fire code requirement in your community. It only makes good sense, anyway, to protect your beautiful, new kitchen from any mishap.

Most restaurant fires start right in the cooking area, progressing to and through the vent to the flue. Careful maintenance, of course, should prevent this from happening to you, but—since we are all human—a fire protection system that will go into action automatically when needed is a must.

At least two hand-sized fire extinguishers of the ABC formula, which puts out *all* kinds of fire—including hot grease—are necessary in your kitchen for smaller emergencies. Place them in a handy spot in your kitchen, but *not* right in the midst of your major cooking equipment.

Refuse Holders

In your kitchen design, don't overlook some space for one or two garbage cans or liner holders where they will be handy to the cook but not obtrusive. This isn't easy, since the containers can't be in your cook's "area of flow," but they can't be placed too far away from the main cooking area either, or the cook will take to throwing things like egg shells in the general vicinity of the garbage. Accuracy will depend on the kind of mood he or she is in—and *that* will vary from day to day.

Microwave Ovens

These have become increasingly more useful in the average restaurant kitchen, since they are now quite reliable and, in addition, fairly rugged. If you plan to utilize one or more, go all out and secure a good-sized model of sufficient capacity to hold at least two beef roasts. Small units will be more bother than they are worth. Check your wiring to make certain you can supply sufficient power for your microwave ovens. They can be wattage hungry.

Electric Mixer

Whether you will need one of these at all will depend primarily on your menu. In general, the more baking you are planning to do, the larger the unit you'll require. If you plan to make and serve doughnuts or pancakes, for example, they are an essential piece of equipment. Otherwise, you will be able to do without.

An electric mixer can be placed virtually anywhere in your kitchen, since it's usually not needed in the rush of meal preparation. I'd recommend your looking for a used model, in stainless steel. They are frequently a very good buy.

Slicing Machine

This is another must in every kitchen, but, again, it needn't occupy crucial serving or preparation space. Get an electric one—the hand-wound ones are a waste of precious time. A blade of from ten to twelve inches in diameter should be sufficient for most of your needs. Don't plan on moving a slicing machine around much, by the way. They are deceptively heavy.

This piece of kitchen equipment is certain to retain bits and pieces of whatever has been sliced, so it will require frequent cleaning. Meats—especially rare meats—can become contaminated within a surprisingly short time in the heat of a kitchen. Plan to clean the slicer after each major use. And be sure to replace the safety guard each time, because that blade is incredibly sharp.

Bun Warmer

This is an optional piece of electric equipment, necessary mostly if you plan to feature hot rolls and breads. It will also moisten somewhat stale breads, cakes, and muffins. One of its greatest charms is that it can be located in an odd corner of your dining room and never be offensive to your patrons. Usually, however, it's to be found near the waiter's stand.

Knife Holder

A knife holder isn't regarded as major equipment by anyone except your cooks who, if they are pros, will take inordinate pride in their collection of knives as a mark and symbol of their profession. Some chefs even carry them along to the job each day in their own attaché cases. Let your cook decide the type, placement, and size needed, and install it wherever he or she wants it. It's a small thing, but sure to please.

You now have your *basic* major equipment for your kitchen. In addition, depending on the kind of restaurant you plan to create, you'll require a soup tureen, baking ovens, poachers, pizza ovens, and the like to fill your specialized prerequisites. You may even want a full soda fountain. Coffee-making machines are frequently placed in an area of the restaurant itself, but you might find it best to design those into your kitchen—although out of the way, please, of your cook. Traditionally, waiters make the coffee in all but the largest of this nation's watering-holes, freeing the cook to do meatier things.

THE DISHWASHING AREA

When planning out your dishwashing space, assume that your restaurant will be a crashing success. You'll need, therefore, a fast follow-up system to keep your dishes, glasses, and silver constantly at the ready. These are the essentials you'll need to consider:

1 dishwashing machine
1 rinse arm
2 drainboards
1 grease trap
2 garbage container holders
1 table
Storage and drainage shelves

1 hot-water heater/booster
Several bus trays and stand
1 to 2 wall fans
Silverware holders
Extra three-position sink
Flooring

Your Dishwashing Machine

Unless your new restaurant is planned to be quite small, and stay that way, an automatic dishwasher will be required at the outset. In some areas of the country, a large three-position sink will meet the health code requirements, provided you install a heater and can keep the rinse temperature in the third and final sink up to 180° F. Check this out first before proceeding.

While methods vary slightly with each manufacturer, the basic principles of an automatic dishwashing machine are the same for almost all. First of all, you have to know that the process *isn't* all automatic. Your staff dishwasher must first manually scrape off leftover foods from the plates into a garbage receptacle, then rinse the platters, glasses, and silverware *before* stacking them into a fitted, drawerlike tray that will, in turn, fit exactly into the body of the machine.

The machine will wash and rinse for you after that— this is really the automatic part. Outside gauges allow your dishwasher to double-check that the wash-cycle temperature and (most importantly) the rinse-cycle temperature are correct. Rinse water must reach 180° F for full sanitation. This temperature also allows for almost immediate drying once the tray is removed with your clean utensils, so, in a sense, this is automatic, too.

Inside the machine, built-in drain trays will catch all debris your first manual cleaning and rinsing may miss. But these trays, in turn, must be emptied fairly often so they don't overflow and clog up the main drain from the machine.

Naturally, a fully licensed plumber or technician will be required to set this machine up and into place for you. He will also install a grease trap as part of your final drainage piping, and this is the third and final catchall for any food debris that is not soluble. Most health codes require one, but if not, insist that a trap be installed anyway. It will save you hundreds of dollars in future plumbing problems and, depending on the size, should not be overly dear. It's another "tremendous trifle."

Proper maintenance, such as we've outlined, will keep your automatic dishwashing machine humming along nicely. Neglect will cost you, both in time and sanitation. Work out a maintenance and cleaning *routine* (write it down and post it on the wall) for your dishwashers to follow, and insist they pay attention.

Automatic dishwashing machines are built by several reputable equipment manufacturers, and come in sizes ranging from frankly too small to huge complexes that more resemble a car wash. Again, judge the size you'll need by your *peak* seating capacity. New ones, while delightful to see in the showrooms, are expensive, and they won't stay new-looking very long once installed and in daily use. So check out any restaurant auctions, or visit a restaurant supply dealer (look in the Yellow Pages) who reconditions and sells previously owned machines. If you can purchase an automatic dishwasher that's less than three or four years old, you'll have a machine that will service your needs very well for years at a bargain price, at least compared to that of a brand-new one. Unless purchased at auction (least expensive of all if you can find one when you need it), insist on a guarantee for as many months as you can get on your used machine. And get it in writing.

Rinse Arm

A rinsing hose is really a part of your dishwashing machine but doesn't always come with it. If one is not provided, purchase a *new* one. It is attached to your sink, on the cleaning and scraping side of your machine. Being part rubber and flexible, it's relatively inexpensive, but expendable. It's a good idea to keep a replacement hose in storage since it *will* wear out fairly soon—and always when your serving staff are at top efficiency, hollering for "more silverware, please."

Drainboards

Surround your dishwashing machine with slightly slanted, stainless-steel drainboards at both ends. Allow at least four feet—more, if possible—for the drainboard at the receiving end, usually the left side. Add to this a standard stainless-steel sink, with a large-capacity drain, over which you will mount that rinse arm we just referred to.

At the other end, the right side, allow space equal to twice the girth of the trays—again, more if practical—for drying.

The drainboards will probably have to be specially made to your individual space requirements. They can be made up for you by a sheet-metal firm, a restaurant sup-

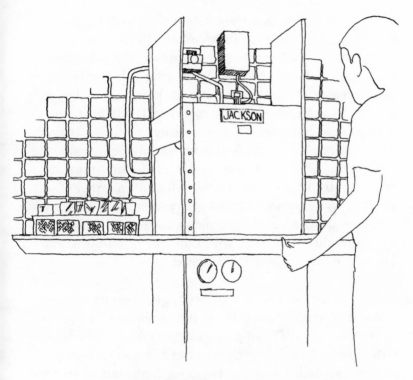

Dishwashing machine with drainboards.

ply firm, or—perhaps easiest of all—they can be cut down to fit from a slightly longer already manufactured piece. Sinks are also stainless steel and come in standard sizes to fit right in.

Garbage Container Holders

The need for easy-to-get-at garbage receptacles is obvious. The handiest are steel frames designed to hold heavy-duty plastic garbage bags. When these bags are filled, they slip out easily and can be tied up and removed. Of course, regular garbage cans can be used, either with

69

or without liners, but they present a constant cleaning problem. And that's an unnecessary time-waster.

A word here about those plastic liners. *Really* heavy-duty bags can be obtained from your wholesale paper goods dealer or restaurant supply house, and they are worth the extra money they cost over the lighter-weight contenders. If these are not readily available in your area, then by all means double up the bags, one inside the other—in your kitchen especially—for maximum strength. Into these receptacles will go all manner of wet, sharp, and heavy foodstuffs—gravy, meat bones, leftover soups, vegetables, coffee grounds—the lot. Don't fill them so thoroughly that they are in danger of bursting when finally tied and ready for removal.

Drain Table and Storage Shelves

As in your kitchen, plan as many shelves as you can. Make them *deep*. Clean pots and pans not in everyday use will inevitably wind up here in the dishwasher's domain, so you can build some of them on high, out of normal reach, as well, or install pot racks overhead.

A general-duty table, in stainless steel or with a hard-plastic table top, is extremely useful if you can find the room for it. If placed between the kitchen and dishwashing areas, both can use it as need be. Extra shelving can be built in below the table top, but off the floor area.

Hot-Water Heater/Booster

Your hot water is supplied, naturally, by your hot-water heater. Sometimes, because of the demands upon its capacity by your dishwashing machine, it will fail to keep a good supply coming to you at all times. No, you don't necessarily have to secure a larger one—check with your plumber or technician to see if a booster, properly installed, might do the same job with your present equipment. Since the demands on your hot-water supply vary at different times during the day, the booster might just be able to carry you when you need it. It's well worth checking into, in all events, before buying another heater.

Keep *both* the booster and the hot-water heater as far away from the dishwashing area as you possibly can. They will radiate a fair amount of unwanted warmth in a spot not especially noted for its cool breezes.

Wall Fans

Install one or two large wall fans directly over or near the dishwashing machine, if possible. Windows (screened, of course) are good, but large fans are better. Your kitchen staff will love you for it.

Silverware Holders

You'll need to secure specially made and health code–approved wire-and-rubber silverware holders (buy at least three, assuming each has six compartments) in which to place your clean silver, handles always *up,* for delivery to the waiters' stand on the floor of the restaurant.

Silver, no matter how well stocked you seem to be, is always in short supply. Capacity use is part of the story. An 80-seat restaurant, fully occupied, will use 240 pieces of silver for each sitting, for example. Silver is easily stolen, and your silverware can just as easily disappear into the garbage bags due to the carelessness of dishwashers or busboys.

To avoid the latter—and this happens far more often than you might imagine in restaurants of every size—

install a special tray or bus box strictly for used silverware. Then require your serving staff and busboys to *separate* the silver from all else when clearing off a table. Put a small quantity of detergent and hot water into the tray and you'll help soak the dirty silver at the same time.

Bus Trays and Stand

Bus trays, no matter what the color, will never be things of beauty. Still, they are an essential part of restaurant life. Keep them in a place by themselves, and out of sight. There are stainless steel carts that will hold several of these; or full ones can be marched directly into the dishwashing area. Plan an inconspicuous corner for your bus trays in your overall avenues of flow.

Extra Three-Position Sink

At least a two-position sink will be a Health Department necessity for use in scouring out pots, frying pans, and other utensils too large or too encrusted to use in your automatic dishwasher. A three-position sink need not be much larger, but it *will* substitute as a dishwashing area should your automatic machine break down. You will need to install a gas jet under the third sink to heat the rinse water, however.

A stainless-steel sink will cost about twice as much as a corrugated steel sink, but will last virtually forever. The cheaper sinks will give service for a few years before needing replacement, so let your initial budget be your guide here. Both will do the job.

Flooring

Finally, consider using rock tiles for your floors in the dishwashing area as well as your kitchen. While vinyl tiles will do, particularly industrial-weight tiles, they will inevitably curl up at the corners in the ever-present dampness, and then trouble will begin. Under *no* circumstances use linoleum or vinyl tiles intended for home use —they are much too thin, and will be thoroughly worn out in just six months.

Installation of non-slip wooden slats in the wet areas of the dishwashing corner is a nice touch as long as they are placed in such a way that no one approaching the area with dishes and glassware is liable to trip on their outer edges. Your own good judgment is best here. Rubber matting might just be better for you.

STORAGE

As a general rule, the more of your supplies you can afford to buy at one time, the cheaper they will be per unit. Every restaurateur buys in quantity, and so will you.

Ah, but this implies ample room to store away the bulk of those orders you will not be using immediately. Strangely enough, as simple a statement as that is, many a restaurant plan has been submitted for approval with storage rooms more resembling broom closets.

To help you to gauge the amount of space you may need, figure on storing away some good quantities of the following:

On Open Shelving
Tinned goods
Spices and sugar
Bottled condiments
Glassware, dishes, etc.

Cereals
Machine and electrical parts
Coffee

In Off-the-Floor Bins
Paper goods
Garbage bags
Soaps
Potatoes
Laundry (one for clean, one for dirty)
Silverware

In Storage Freezers
Meats (especially hamburger)
Portion-controlled entrées
French fries
Frozen juices and vegetables
Frozen fish
Extra bread and rolls

In Storage Refrigerators or Walk-In Box
Beer in kegs
Some poultry
Produce
Citrus fruits
Eggs and butter
Milk

In Liquor Room
Beer by the case
Pouring wine by the case
Wines by the bottle

Liquors
Setups or extra tanks
Bar supplies

The lists above are included *only* to serve as a general outline for you in determining the storage space you'll require. Starting with these lists, make your own tally, adding and subtracting as you calculate what you'll need for your own menu. Then plan accordingly. I've never known a restaurateur to complain that he had too much storage room.

The size of the walk-in refrigerator room should be settled first, since it's the most important and will take the most space.

Basements, of course, are ideal for *long-term* storage of almost everything, and a natural for beer, wines, and liquors. However, keep your foodstuffs and liquors well apart from the rooms or areas containing your compressor motors and hot-water heaters, since they generate a fair amount of heat all the time.

Your local health regulations will undoubtedly require that virtually *everything* except mopheads be kept up off the floor, so design your shelving that way from the beginning.

Freezers and refrigerators come in all sizes and heights. If you plan to use your basement, measure carefully all doors, passageways or step clearances down there to be sure that the equipment you want to order can, in fact, be gotten *in* without tearing out the walls.

Dressing rooms—one for the women, one for the men —can be located in storage areas provided you can afford the space. Be sure to install a healthy lock on each door, however, for all those obvious reasons that just flashed through your mind. A listing of the basic furnishings needed for dressing rooms is included at the back of the book. Use it as a guide.

PLUMBING, HEATING, AND WIRING

It is in this area that the average restaurateur feels the least knowledgeable.

Not so. Not really. You, for example, probably already know a fair bit about drains, air-conditioning units, the old furnace, and, perhaps, something about simple wiring. After all, didn't you rewire Aunt Samantha's bridge lamp for her?

The plumbing, heating, and wiring in your new restaurant is essentially the same as those that exist in your home, except there's a lot more of it. Pipes still carry hot and cold water; and some motors have been taken right out of the refrigerators, for instance, in order to function better at a cool distance.

Everything that is done, however, makes good sense. Soon you will find yourself understanding it all, wondering, at the conclusion—when the last wire is stretched, the last wrench turned—why in the world you were once so bearish about it all.

We'll start right now. Let's take a look at these things:

Air conditioning
Heating
Compressors
Hot-water heater/booster
Piping, venting, and drainage
Spillover sink
Wiring

Air Conditioning

Always seek out the advice of experts in this field unless you are extraordinarily well versed yourself. Your contractor or architect should be able to guide you to the right system for your climate, projected usage, and other variables. There are no simple rules to follow here except to suggest that you secure two or three opinions from qualified technicians before making any decisions.

Basically, your choices come down to individual in-wall air-conditioning units vs. a central system.

It can be argued that for a moderately large restaurant, 125 seats or more, a central air-conditioning unit is preferable to several individual wall units. Certainly it will be cheaper to run; if you're in a warm climate, that may be the end of the discussion. A central unit cools more quickly, as well.

With smaller restaurants, large in-wall air-conditioning units may be preferable, especially if your needs will only be seasonal. Wall units are cheaper to buy and install than a central system, and it is highly unlikely that they'll *all* fail at any one time. A full restaurant does put a strain on them, however, so you'll have to know the number of BTUs you'll require to cool your place effectively. That magic number will depend, mostly, on the size of your place (including the height of the ceiling) so get your square-footage facts at the ready from your blueprints. With this at hand, you can then intelligently discuss the number and size units you'll want with your sales people.

If an air-conditioning system is already installed in the building, bully for you. But be sure to have all the equipment thoroughly inspected, and parts replaced if necessary, before sending out any opening night invitations.

Heating

If you must install your own heating plant, you will *have* to seek professional advice—preferably from your own architect or contractor. What you decide to install will depend on the climate, availability, initial installation costs, and fuel. You may be able to utilize your air-conditioning ducting for forced air, or plug into a city steam service. Your local heating specialists will have these answers for you. Talk to them *all* and weigh the advantages.

Again, as always, try for the maximum guarantees you can get before placing any orders for either heating or air-conditioning units. Frequently, your suppliers will offer a maintenance contract. If so, read over the terms carefully; in general, however, these contracts are well worth the small monthly costs.

Compressors

Your walk-in refrigerator room, freezers, and individual refrigerators and lowboys all work with compressor motors. They are small electric engines, each with a large fan belt. If your units are self-contained (like the one in your own kitchen at home), the compressor is built right into the machine, usually at the bottom. If not, the motor is separated from the refrigerating box but connected to it by wires and piping; it usually resides in the basement or other out-of-the-way spot.

Any place you locate them, however, *must* have sufficient cooling air space all around them. They run day and night, and will get hot. Actually, a basement floor is ideal, since it's normally cool—and that's where you'll find compressors in most restaurants.

One motor, if it's large enough, can sometimes do the

work for two refrigerating units. It's a nice saving on electricity, but ask your electrician to make *certain* there's ample power there to do the job.

Provide adequate light in your compressor area so that adjustments can be made from time to time to keep them in good running order. Never crowd them together.

Finally, make certain your electrician provides you with an automatic thermal cutoff for these machines. Since compressors can overheat if out of adjustment, this simple installation will afford you peace of mind during the hours when your place is closed.

Hot-Water Heater/Booster

Whether gas or electric, it is *most* important that you ascertain that your hot-water tank has a capacity large enough to supply your guzzling dishwashing machine. This will be your biggest hot-water user by far. Check that out first, to avoid securing an outsized one (wasteful) or undersized unit. In some instances a booster heater will be needed to supply your dishwashing machine with water consistently hot enough (180° F) for the rinse cycle. Therefore, consult with *both* your dishwasher technician and your plumber before you purchase your hot-water tank.

Piping, Venting, and Drainage

Here again, use your good common sense. There will always be local building code requirements for commercial plumbing, drain sizes, and venting allowances. Therefore, try to learn as much as you can about them so you can discuss your needs with your plumber contractor in a manner that will gain his respect. Primarily this means not to ask him to do gymnastics with your piping

—remember, a building inspector has to approve his work before you can open.

Shortcuts are well named. To avoid this, double-check your plumber's work each day to make certain that what is going in is exactly what you asked for. Often the actual plumber doing the work in your place is not the one you talked with, but an associate. Don't be overly surprised, then, if the work varies from what you anticipated. If it does, find out why. If you don't like it, don't let him continue.

Plumbers may have good singing voices but are rarely artistic. They'll run pipes in the wildest places if you don't spell out for them *exactly* where they are to be placed.

Eliminate guesswork. Buy most of your basic equipment for your kitchen, dishwashing area, walk-in refrigerator room, and bar *before* your plumber starts his work.

As a final double-check before the plumber leaves your premises (never to be found again short of ten days prior notice), have him personally show you where *all* the cutoff valves are, and explain their function to you. They'll be in out-of-the-way places that defy the normal imagination in some cases. Color code them yourself, with a chart you can hang up on the wall (with a duplicate for your office files). Be sure you know where the master cutoff valve is for water and gas, and exactly how to use it if ever necessary.

Spillover Sink

Known in some circles as a "slop sink"—and not a bad description at that—this is a final checkpoint for your drainage before it goes into the main. It's important, even if not lovely to look at. It will require periodic cleaning out, since any oversized waste material will probably clog up here, where you—and not your plumber—can readily get at it. Inspect it daily and see that it's kept clear.

Wiring

Unless you hire a *licensed* electrician (they are registered and have state-supplied numbers) you will probably not be able to secure a buildings permit to allow you to open. Since proper wiring is downright essential to you, don't even *think* of skimping here, even if good ole Uncle Oscar tells you he can easily do it for you at half price after dark.

Again, buy as much of your electrical equipment, including light fixtures, as you can before your electricians begin work. They can also provide outlets for you, in some cases, where you know you'll need them, and return later for final follow-up. Still, they work by the hour and are downright expensive, so use their services as efficiently as you can by having your electrical layout and actual fixtures ready for installation at one time.

Your fuse box—or, more likely, your circuit breakers, —can be mounted on the wall in a convenient place for you—but not a customer—to get to it when needed. Plan this out in advance, or it'll wind up perched behind your freezer. Then type up a sheet, similar to the one you made for the valves, code it, and place it on the wall or the inner cover of the circuit breaker box.

Finally, insist—and I cannot emphasize this too strongly—that your electricians provide you with an accessible master cutoff switch for emergencies. You'd be astounded how many restaurateurs haven't the foggiest idea where that is, or if they even have one.

GARBAGE DISPOSAL

A nasty by-product of all restaurants is garbage. In most communities, a private cartage company will have to be engaged, and you'll have to pay to get rid of it.

On your part, however, you will have to bag it, containerize it, stack it—somehow make it easy to be picked up. In America our garbage has to be *neat*, see?

If there is access for a truck to get to the rear of your restaurant, that's where you'll want to house it all. Given the space, create and *fence in* a garbage area back there; try to keep it some distance from your restaurant building itself if you possibly can. Put down a cement floor inside the garbage area for easy cleaning and simple stability.

On the other hand, if your garbage has to be picked up from the street side, then you'll have to construct an outside bin in which to hold it until it's collected. Its size depends, of course, on the seating of your establishment, but don't skimp when building the bin—it will fill up *instantly*. On a variation of a well-known "law," garbage expands to fill up its containers. A top-opening bin is easiest (since gravity will help hold the lid down), but design the sides no higher than four to four and a half feet for ease in the actual handling of the individual garbage bags. They can get awfully heavy. Schedule the bin for a daily check, and clean up after your collectors have departed. They always leave a little something to remember them by.

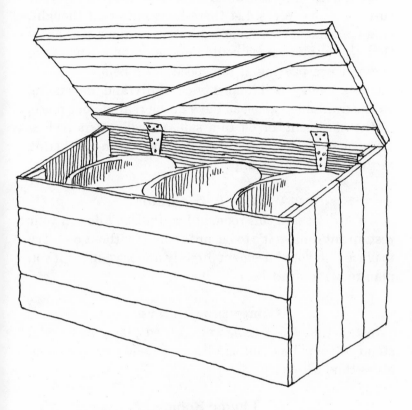

Garbage bin box.

AUXILIARY ROOMS OR AREAS

At one time or another in this chapter we have referred to various extra rooms in your new restaurant that help keep it functioning smoothly. A short recap here will help you to keep perspective.

It's the out-of-sight rooms and hidden areas—each with

83

their special functions and all humming away—that make the art of restaurateuring look so effortless to your customers and peers. Let them hang onto that thought. However, like a captain of a great ocean liner, *you* know that the public rooms couldn't even exist without the engine room purring at top speed down below.

Check over your blueprints carefully and, depending on the available space you have in the rear of your place, in the basement, or off to a side, parcel out individual areas or rooms as follows. I'll try to put down this listing in the order of most importance:

Walk-In Refrigerator

We've discussed this room at length. Don't design your restaurant (unless it's to be quite small) without one. Try to place it in your basement directly under your bar if you plan to serve draft beer.

Compressor Motors

Install these in a cool, well lighted place, in a small stand of their own, on the floors. Provide for plenty of access and air space.

Liquor Room

Large or small, as your needs will be, but be sure the room sports a metal door with a solid lock on it.

Ice Machine

This invaluable machine can be fitted into any of several vacant corners or along a hallway, although most are surprisingly large overall. Remember, I recommend *renting* the machine.

Sizes will vary, as usual, depending on your requirements. The machine will make ice cubes for you of varying sizes as well as crushed ice. If you plan a bar, or just a fair-sized restaurant, you'll need one.

Hot-Water Heater/Booster
We've covered this piece of equipment pretty thoroughly, too, in this chapter. However, be sure to position the tank and the booster, if you need one, *by themselves,* since they radiate a good bit of heat. Provide air spaces, and an overhead light in order to check out the temperature, or reset.

Auxiliary Freezers and Refrigerators
Try to position them near your walk-in refrigerator room so that transfer from one to the other is simplified. Install as many as you can on the theory that—especially in very hot weather—one will always be out of commission.

Linen Storage
You'll need a special bin or set of shelves for your fresh linen, and a bin or two for the dirty stuff. Keep your fresh linen covered, or in their packages, until needed.

Shelving for Tinned/Bottled Foods
Even tinned foods must be kept well off the floor, on shelves. If you build them about three inches away from the walls, as well, you will surprise and delight your health inspector.

Use hard plastic, stainless steel, wire shelving, or enamel any wooden shelves. Never use shelf paper or a stick-down covering—in fact, use no covering whatever. Install an overhead light so you can read the labels easily.

When you place a new order of food supplies on any shelf, put them toward the back, bringing up to front position those cans and bottles that were there before. In this very simple way you will be automatically assured that no foodstuffs will remain with you longer than they ought.

Dressing Rooms

Separate rooms, well lighted, with locks on the doors, are a splendid accommodation for your staff if you have the space. Furnish the rooms with a chair or two, many hangers and hooks, a shelf, and a large full-length mirror.

Closet

Into this room you can stow away those ubiquitous mops, mopheads, brooms and pails. Store your soaps, tools, and your cleaning/painting supplies in here, out of the way of the general run of the restaurant.

Fire Extinguishers

Keep at least four mounted on the wall in convenient places. One should be installed near the stairway, one near the compressor motors, one in the general shelving area, and one near the hot water tank. *Near.* Not adjacent, however. This should comply with your local fire laws.

Your individual extinguishers must be inspected by your fire protection people (the same ones who will inspect your kitchen hood automatic extinguisher setup) every six months. Set up a schedule with them. Call them any time, however, for refills should you ever have occasion to use an extinguisher. The service is not expensive, particularly in view of the protection offered.

DINING ROOM

We've saved the best for last. Here, of all the rooms in your new restaurant, you can—at last—exercise your own ingenuity. Expect this part to be fun. It ought to be —after all, this is the room your customers and friends will come to know and enjoy with you again and again.

Here is a listing of the equipment (depending of course upon the kind of restaurant) you'll want to consider for this room. *How* you put it together—the decor you choose, the very placement of tables, chairs, and lights— these are for you, and you alone, to decide. You don't need a handbook for creativity, and none would do you justice anyway.

However, you *will* have to be able to fit in most of the following into your plan-of-flow:

Booths, tables and chairs
Table lamps and overhead lighting
Table coverings and service
Floor coverings
Counter and stools
Stand-up, glass-fronted refrigerator
Ice cream soda fountain
Coffee maker and stand
Powder rooms
Waiters' stand
Pass-through counter
Salad bar

General considerations for areas of easy flow
Nice extra touches

Booths, Tables and Chairs—or Both?

If you are fortunate enough to be blessed with space, opt for at least *some* booths or banquettes. They allow for a measure of privacy (or the appearance of it anyway!), they are invariably comfortable and cozy, and as such they will be the preferred seating on your floor.

If space is at a premium—more often the case, unfortunately—try utilizing banquette seating of the type that runs continuously along one wall. In front of these can be placed square tables of any length, with chairs on the outside.

Small square tables suitable for two should be ordered in uniform sizes so that two or three or more of them can

Square table with fold-down edges.

be placed together if needed for a larger party. In addition, full-size square tables seating four can be made up for you with folded-down rounded edges on each end; these can be propped up when needed to form a larger round table suitable for five or six people.

A word to the wise: Don't neglect to provide *some* tables for solitary diners. If you don't, your single customers will only take a larger table or booth to themselves, and that's not only embarrassing, it's downright uneconomic.

Sometimes a truly delightful nook can be engineered out of an unlikely space. An oversized closet not needed, or the space under a stairway to an upper floor is ideal for a cozy booth—the odder the shape in this case, the better. Take a good look at your blueprints with this in mind. I know a pancake house in a college town that utilized such a space under a stairway to create a triangular-shaped table around a pillar. It was surrounded by a specially built triangular-shaped booth that seated ten to twelve people. It was always crowded, even preferred!

Table Coverings and Service

Creativity is certainly the key word here. Assuming that you'll want your restaurant to express your own individuality and taste, this is one of the most intimate areas for your consideration. Your table coverings, indeed, can become part of your decor itself if—for example —they express cool chic in sparkling white or pastel hues, or the relaxed hospitality of red-and-white-checked tablecloths. Polished wood, table mats, inlaid wood panels on your tabletops, or butcher blocks all articulate your taste, and go a long way toward helping you to create the mood you desire.

So do your individual choices of dishes, silver service, and napkins. Your range of choices here is incredible, and need only be limited by your budget. Try to secure some catalogs from your local restaurant supply house or, best of all, go there and look them over. You and you alone know your limits here.

In general, though, provide two and a half times the seating capacity of your new restaurant in volume for silver, regular dishes, salad bowls, cups and saucers, and table glasses. Buy considerably less of such items as soup bowls, egg cups, monkey dishes (small, six-inch-diameter bowls), dessert plates, and other less-in-demand dishes depending, naturally, on your own menu. Remember that all these items *will* be broken or worn out, probably within a year or two. As much as possible, then, buy from *open* stock at your supplier's. You'll be astounded at the variety readily available, but don't be carried away with unusual shapes or patterns that will be hard to duplicate later.

On the other hand, if your budget is slim, try the auctions again or investigate those houses in your restaurant supply district that have bought out restaurants at auction. Here the best rule is simplicity. Try to choose your dishes in a single color. White is the most plentiful, and all cooked entrées look good when served on white platters. If you have to mix patterns to get the quantity you need, the single color hue is even more advised. You'll be surprised how few people will notice a diversity of pattern if the dishes are all the same color.

Much the same is true of silver. If your restaurant is to be in a popular, high-turnover area, your silverware pilferage will be, sorry to say, proportionate. In this instance, then, simply buy the least expensive "silver" that will do the job for you without bending, and plan frequent reorders. Even the more expensive restaurants feature quite ordinary salt and pepper shakers on their tables these days. Can you guess why?

Cloth napkins are at least a modest sign of luxury, and certain classes of restaurants simply must have them. You can buy or make your own or—as with tablecloths, too—arrange with a commercial laundry in your area to deliver and pick up their own line on a regular basis. This method is the simplest and surest for most restaurants. Check out at least one or two firms if you can, not only for any pricing variations, but for delivery schedules and quality before you make your selections.

Paper napkins and paper mats are available in dozens of sizes and folds. They can be printed up for you in dazzling colors, using one of the printer's designs or one of your own. Costs will depend almost entirely on the size of the order you are prepared to give, and the frequency of reorders you anticipate. Because of its easy disposability, paper is almost always preferred for fast-turnover restaurants. If you intend to use napkin holders on your tables, you'll be wise to check with your paper suppliers to see if they will provide these for you—*free.*

Table Lamps

Candles,* candle lamps, or individual table lamps all contribute enormously to a mood of contentment and compatability, and are, therefore, highly recommended for all types of restaurants. Gone—thank heaven—are

*Be sure to check with your fire department—and your insurance agent—before installing any candle lighting.

the days of the overhead fluorescent tubes under which everyone, patron and server alike, looked hungover. Even our largest fast-food chains have begun to appreciate the value (and the relatively small cost) of table lighting to their clientele.

Americans and most Europeans share a charming peculiarity in that we all seek a feeling of intimacy in our public dining rooms. We tend to leave the garish lights to the truck stops, fading hamburger joints, and probably our own kitchen sinks. When we dine out—whatever the cuisine or price—we want it to be, above all, cozy.

Be prepared for a bit of frustration in this area, however. Coziness does *not* come easily, and you must experiment in your own premises—over and over, if necessary —with all your lighting. Try a variety of individual lamps if you can. Explore all the variables—the effects of various light wattages, size and color of shades, on-table or overhead—*before* placing your order. Don't be rushed. Lighting is just too important to the success of your restaurant to be done hurriedly. Check the effects at night as well as during the day, to be certain the lights you choose will work for you equally well each time. Be tenacious in this. Many a good restaurant fails to live up to its decor simply because the lighting is wretchedly wrong for it.

A dimmer for all overhead lights is a *must;* these you lower, strangely enough, after dark.

When you have at last achieved the full effect you want, you can be understandably proud of your efforts. You will have gone a long way in finally providing the setting you've dreamed of for your own restaurant.

Floor Covering

What a marvelous range you have to choose from here, from treated sawdust all the way to deep nylon piling.

Select whatever flooring is consistent with the overall character of your dining room, bearing in mind that whatever it may be, you will have to undertake to get it cleaned each night of its life. Real carpeting, for example, will require an investment in a machine to soap it and clean it. Hardwood floors or inlaid industrial tiles are considerably easier and less bothersome to keep clean, and need nothing more than the old-fashioned mop and pail (and a good industrial-strength liquid soap) to keep it that way. Given normal wear, both should last you about five years or more, depending pretty much on your area's climate.

Never attempt to utilize linoleum or plastic tiles made for home use. They will wear out completely within six months or so and, worse, will *begin* to show wear after only about two months of traffic. Only thick industrial tiles print the pattern below the surface, usually. I *know* the home tile patterns are beautiful, and they look especially inviting in those glossy catalogs. Nevertheless, don't be tempted.

Counter with Stools

Counters, if you plan to use one, can be purchased already made or custom built; or your own carpenter can build one for you. They are relatively simple and should pose no particular problem for you. Whatever you choose to do, make the design of the counter top consistent with the tops of the rest of your tables (unless they're to be covered with cloths) so that everything in your restaurant is all of a pattern and fits together.

Below the counter top you will have ample space for shelving and upright areas for garbage bag stands. Under the counter is a splendid place to position a small sink. Install it near your fountain, so you can utilize the same basic drains.

If you feature a counter, place one end of it as near to the front doorway as possible. Counters are used, normally, by singles or parties in a bit of a hurry, so make it easy for these folk to sit down and, presumably, be quickly served. If prospective customers have to wind their way through a labyrinth, or cross a crowded room, they'll turn around and leave—and you'll have lost some good, perhaps steady, patrons.

You can affix your counter stools fairly close to each other only if they have no back rests or arms. Otherwise, place them about a yard apart, with side-swinging seats.

Since your counter stools will have to sustain an almost constant workout, buy the best quality and workmanship you can find. If they're to be affixed to the floor, make absolutely certain that they are bolted in as *securely* as you can to avoid the wobblies.

Stand-Up Glass-Fronted Refrigerator

This is about a four-foot-wide serving refrigerator, usually mounted atop another, lowboy refrigerator, that will be placed in your dining room if your plans include a counter. Install it along the wall alongside your coffee stand or ice cream soda fountain because it will get a lot of hard, daily use. In this glass-fronted refrigerator you can keep your freshly made salad and all its fixings, juices, and an assortment of desserts that have to be maintained at a cool temperature. The glass doors, incidentally, will be slightly slanted, and on rollers, so that they will close by themselves. Don't even *consider* buying a refrigerator without this feature.

Ice Cream Soda Fountain

Are you planning to feature America's favorite dessert, ice cream? Good. Place your soda fountain equipment opposite your counter area. It will function remarkably like a regular liquor bar, after which it is somewhat modeled.

For a complete soda bar setup you will require:

1 fountain
1 ice-making machine and 1 ice bin
1 to 2 soda and other dispensers
1 to 2 milkshake machines or equivalent
1 coffee stand and brewer

Except for the ice machine, try to secure all these in previously used and rebuilt condition if your budget is getting thin, since the cost of new fountain equipment can be a bit stiff. Fortunately, it should be relatively easy for you to do this, using the regular restaurant supply sources we've discussed so far. This maneuver is doubly worthwhile for you, since relatively few innovations have been made in basic fountain equipment over the last ten years.

The Fountain What a grand name for this piece of equipment! From it *does* flow all kinds of good things that appeal, these days, to all ages.

Like all restaurant equipment, fountains come in a large variety of sizes. But all of them will contain freezer slots for bulk ice cream containers, and the number of these you will require usually determines the overall dimensions of your fountain. They will also have built-in seltzer and fresh water overhand taps, ice cream scoop rests, a drain, and several containers—some refrigerated and with covers—for flavored syrups, cherries, marshmallow toppings, and other mouth-watering condiments. It must be made of stainless steel for easy—and well-nigh constant—wiping up. Once in place, you'll need the services of both an electrician and a plumber for final hookup. Be sure the drains from your fountain are large enough not to clog up easily (ice cream tends to clog). Try to locate your seltzer tanks directly below the fountain in the basement or as close as possible.

It's a dream come true. Haven't you always—be honest now—ever since you were a wee child, *always* wanted your *own* ice cream fountain?!!

Ice-Making Machine We've discussed the pros and cons of purchasing vs. renting this machine earlier in this chapter. An ice bin under the counter, with a protective, movable cover, will often be quite sufficient for your fountain uses, unless your soft-drink trade is unusually heavy. The bin can be refilled as needed from your ice-making machine located in an out of the way spot.

Soda Dispensers In addition to plain drinking and seltzer water, you will need a dispenser or two that holds the various heady soft-drink syrups to blend with that seltzer. Some soft-drink manufacturers will still supply you with these dispenser machines, but most these days require you to buy them, even though they are specially designed for their own product, and advertise it. Try to secure one that will hold at least three different syrups, and, since they're so popular now, plan to serve some "diet" sugarless drinks.

If you can design these dispensers for placement near or adjacent to your basic fountain, you should be able to utilize the same drains.

Other Dispensers Most full-service soda fountains require a milk dispenser. This is basically a small refrigerator, often set up on the back counter itself, into which large containers of milk can be placed, with a pouring spigot at the bottom. These functional dispensers work on the gravity system and allow you to measure out the exact amounts of milk you need; this is invaluable when you are busy, and all but essential to most counter setups. Often your milk suppliers will furnish you with this piece of equipment free of charge (just use their dairy!), so shop around.

You'll probably need, in addition, an iced-tea dispenser, a hot chocolate machine, and a refrigerated unit to mix and dispense fruit juices. All should be measured and designed to fit into your back counter, and as close together as possible to keep your piping and electrical work in one area.

Milkshake Machine Unless you propose to use any of the several "frostee"-type shakes, you'll need a genuine milkshake machine that combines ice cream, syrup, and milk into a truly quality product. These machines are built as single units, all the way to five or six on one stand, each with its own motor. Since the cost here is not all that great, I'd recommend securing a new machine, unless you can find one that hasn't really seen much wear recently.

97

Keep your equipment clean, wipe it down *whenever* it overflows (don't ever try to make *two* milk shakes in one container), and it will serve you well. Milkshakes and malteds are very nice profit items.

Coffee Stand and Brewer Many restaurateurs prefer to place their coffee urns or automatic coffee makers on the back counter for easy access. If you plan no counter, the large urns are best placed in the kitchen, out of sight, or in an area of your dining room least likely to be seen by your patrons. An automatic coffee machine, however, displaying pots of freshly brewed coffee, *is* fairly attractive, not obtrusive, and can easily be made a part of your waiters' stand.

A large seating capacity, unfortunately, limits your use of automatic coffee makers—they simply cannot make fresh coffee fast enough without someone in almost constant attendance. Urns can provide you with very good coffee *provided* you do not leave your coffee in the urns, constantly heating, all day long, and provided you clean out the urns frequently. If you do this, your urns will serve you well, and be constantly at the ready for you, particularly during your rush hours. Make coffee as often as you can, so that it is as fresh as possible—never make a large quantity when you open, and expect to heat and serve it all day long. Coffee itself can "burn," which is what has happened when it tastes bitter to you regardless of the amount of sugar you put into it. Boiling also separates the oils, and turns your coffee into a witch's brew.

For smaller restaurants—eighty or under, let's say— automatic coffee machines are advised, since the coffee is made a pot at a time and is, therefore, always fresh. And you'll never have to throw out any more than one pot at the end of the day.

Here, too, check with the wholesaler who will supply you with your coffee. There are usually three blends to choose from, each one richer than the former, and each costing a bit more. Try all the blends in your own machines first, if you can, before deciding which is best for your own operation. Then, too, your coffee wholesaler may provide you with the *loan* of an automatic coffee-making machine (*and* repair it whenever it needs it!) for as long as you continue to buy from that company.

Powder Rooms

A century or two ago this phrase probably referred to wigs and such; now it means good old soap powder—and is essential. Only a few words of advice will be given here, since this area is somewhat personal—and much usually depends on your available space.

Some cities or states will *require* two separate restrooms for men and women, so check this out first with the Buildings Department in your community. (A *small* restaurant can often make do with a single restroom.) Keep the rooms relatively small, design them for easy cleanup —use rock tile flooring, if possible—and keep them uncluttered. Provide no more than is necessary, actually, unless you plan an attendant, since these rooms will generate no income whatever for you. In the men's room, avoid urinals unless they are already in place; they are ungainly, odorous, and difficult to keep flushed and clean. Keep extra supplies of toweling and paper close at hand for replacement when needed in a hurry. The Health Department will require you to mount a sign in both rooms that reads: "Employees must wash their hands after each use of this room." Do it, and make sure, as best you can, that *they* do it, too.

Waiters' Stand

This is a catchall designation given to a fair-sized table or set of shelves or sideboard near the food serving area. In or around it will be found the tools your waiters and waitresses will need for efficient service, such as:

    A water fountain
    Glasses
    Silverware in trays
    Napkins in bins
    Condiments and sauces in individual bottles
    Extra plates
    Peppermills and extra salt shakers
    Fresh sponges and cleanup rags
    Teabags and individual decaffeinated coffee packets
    Extra sugar packets and packaged crackers

In addition, your waiter's stand might also incorporate any of the following:

    The coffee machine
    Hot water (or a warming burner)
    Bun warmer oven
    Cups and saucers
    Salad in trays on ice
    Salad dressing pourers
    Salad bowls
    Juices on ice or in a refrigerator

Juice glasses

A mounted copy of the day's menu

Pass-Through Counter

If you and your help are not to go into the kitchen area itself to pick up completed orders, you'll have to construct a pass-through counter area on the dining room side of the kitchen chef's domain. In some restaurants, a whole wall is given over to this function, making the kitchen an integral part of the restaurant floor itself. This is a nice touch provided you build your counter *high* enough so your patrons see only the heads and shoulders of your cooks, and *nothing* of their preparation areas, preserving your patron's illusions of a perfectly orderly kitchen back there.

Otherwise, try to design the floor of your dining room in such a way that the pass-through counter is out of the mainstream of your patron's tables or booths. Sometimes it might be advisable to erect a single wall-like structure, behind which your staff can go to pick up their orders. In any case, you want your customers to be surprised and delighted when their entrees arrives before they have spotted them waiting to be picked up.

The overhead warming lights—necessary and integral to your pass-through counter—must be screened from view in the restaurant itself, since they tend to overwhelm all the other lighting you have so thoughtfully provided to create your mood.

Structure your waiters' stand, coffee machines, and water fountain (your bar may provide the latter) as near as possible to the pass-through area for total efficiency, naturally.

Salad Bar

With enough space and easy areas of flow for your patrons to walk about, a self-serve salad bar is a delight for your customers and staff alike. Breads and rolls can also be provided there—it will actually prove out to be cheaper, since adults tend to go easy on breads, and only children take more than they can possibly eat.

Keep the salad bar area free of any obstructions, and place tables and chairs a fair distance away. Your patrons are not waiters—their sense of balance is often less than sure, especially after a glass or two of Old Panther Fizz.

There are refrigerated salad tables on the market, and they are excellent. Otherwise, large, fairly shallow trays lined with chipped ice will do the trick so long as they are frequently drained and the melted ice replaced with fresh. Plan on doing that just as often as you replace the salad fixings. Use small pitchers for your dressings, with narrow, slow-pouring lips, and label each in large, easy-to-see letters to avoid confusion.

General Considerations for Areas of Easy Flow

However you lay out your dining room, you must provide for areas of flow—a self-explanatory phrase that, brought down to cases, simply means not to overcrowd your tables and chairs so that both your patrons and servers have to walk an obstacle course. If your space is limited, this becomes a major problem for you, as you'll discover the minute you begin putting your tables in.

Before doing that, then, photocopy a couple dozen (yes, *dozen*) pages of a hand drawing of the layout of your dining room floor. Do the drawing yourself, with a good ruler, and keep it to *exact* scale. Show all the little indents and corners, electrical outlets, as well as doors, windows, or any other built-in obstructions. Using the same scale, make cutouts of your tables, chairs, stools, and booths, and move them about *on paper*. You'll save a lot of sore muscles this way, yet accomplish the same thing.

Among the facts you'll want to consider in your layout are these:

- Aisles between tables, by law in most states, must be three feet wide at least. It's a good rule, probably originally promulgated by the fire department.
- You'll need to allow another three feet each time you fit in a chair. It takes that extra foot at a minimum to slide a two-foot-deep chair back and forth.
- Keep the area clear around your pass-through counter and/or double doors leading into your kitchen. Nobody wants to sit there anyway.
- If the climate in your area is severe, even for a few months, you may need to build in a small vestibule (approximately three by four and a half feet) off your front door—with a second door or set of double doors, swinging, leading into the restaurant proper, to help keep out the cold. Consolidate this little room into your plan, if need be, but then don't place any tables too close to it. If space is really limited, you might be allowed to build this vestibule *outside*.
- Always place your liquor bar or counter near to the front door so your patrons can reach it with ease.

- Set aside one end of your liquor bar for the exclusive use of your serving staff. They have to be able to order and pick up the booze served at all your tables, and they won't appreciate one bit having to compete with your customers for the bartender's eye. If need be, erect a set of handsome—but effective—brass bars that will mark off the "waiters' stand" end of your bar.

Nice Extra Touches

To help distinguish your place from any other restaurants catering to the same crowd, try to incorporate any number of individual, personal touches. They might include:

- Fresh flowers on every table
- Crackers and cheese or *fresh* peanuts on the bar
- Magazines and newspapers on a handy shelf or rack
- Hanging plants
- Specially folded napkins
- Music or muted jukebox
- Matches as well as an ashtray at each table
- Complimentary after-dinner mints
- Unique outside sign or lighting that can become a trademark
- If zoning allows, tables outside when the weather is pleasant

THE AUCTION ROUTE

It may help you to know that in most major cities throughout the United States, auctions of restaurant equipment, tables, chairs, cash registers, fountains, air conditioners, complete bar service, and the like are constantly being held. Check your local or nearby newspapers, especially the Friday through Sunday editions, under the "Auctions" heading. Often very good equipment—at the most, needing a good, thorough cleaning or re-gasketing—can be purchased (for cash, however) at a fraction of its initial cost. Thus, with moderate luck and a bit of smart bidding, you might be able to assemble a $25,000 kitchen, quite complete and in good order, for about $8,000. It happens every day. By all means at least give it a try.

Some dealers in *new* kitchen equipment may allow you an installment payment plan on the condition that you place most of your equipment business with them. That may work out quite favorably for you, and it is worth asking the dealer about *before* you actually make any purchases. If you go this route, however, be certain to compare prices to assure you that you're not paying a premium for the installment services that is exorbitant.

9

DESIGNING YOUR INTERIOR AND EXTERIOR "LOOK"

Whether you will require the services of a skilled designer for your new restaurant should depend not only on your budget, but, primarily, on your personal skill at creating and projecting the exact appearance you have in mind right now. It seems an easy task at first. Unfortunately, it is not.

Almost everyone just *knows* that he or she is a made-in-heaven, natural-born designer. Aunt Henrietta, who did such wonders redecorating her old sewing room, will be right in there with her fruitful suggestions. Most, however, rarely go beyond the "hanging plants" stage, or color-coordination ideas. They are totally at a loss when it comes down to designing maximum seating, legal passageways, back bars, or areas of flow.

If you yourself are truly adept at conveying your structural and decorating plans to a contractor, you can probably save the cost of a designer. If not—or even if you're in doubt—it's best to seek outside assistance, someone who can understand your ideas and give them back to you in a practical, workable form. Select one or two, confer with them, and ask for some roughs. Most will be happy to do this for you as a way of bidding for the job. Decor is so very important to the success of your new venture that a few dollars saved by going it alone in this area can be sheer folly.

An architect/engineer is not the same, by the way, as a designer. *His* function is to translate your and your designer's ideas into workable blueprints for your contractor. In addition, he will advise you on the latest local and federal laws governing structural changes, caution you regarding materials that can and cannot be used in a public place, and—if necessary—see that your plans are approved by the Buildings Department. He know the heights at which you can install equipment—your outside flue, for example—and can help you secure the proper power from the local electric and gas company. As such, he can save you a hundred headaches.

Ask the owners of the newer businesses in your neighborhood who they used, or consult with your local contractor. A good architect/engineer is a *must*.

After you have designed your kitchen and serving areas, look next to your dining room. Choose a style that will complement your cuisine if you can—for example, French Provincial for a Continental menu, or a hunting lodge "look" for a pancake house. Whatever style you elect, try to keep your basic decor as uncluttered as possible. It will all get dusty in hard-to-clean places as well as smoke impregnated after a very few months. Since keeping your dining room clean is downright essential, design it so that cleaning is a fairly easy task. Avoid knobby-textured wallpaper, or rough cloth walls and drapes, since dust and dirt will tend to cling to them. Avoid too-bright basic colors; they can become awfully tiring after a short time. Imagine your own dining room at home after hundreds of people each day have tramped through it! Now design your new room in the restaurant with that thought in mind.

General advice in the decorating area is limited by its very nature. No two problems are exactly the same. Certain advice is always true. Try to choose a clean, unique "look" for your dining room. Be original. Never attempt a variation of the decor of another local establishment, no matter how much you may admire it. You will want your patrons to form a good impression of your *own* arrangements and, as important, to *remember* it.

Much can be accomplished with interior paint colors, and pictures or mirrors placed strategically along the walls. Obtrusive pillars can be mirrored or paneled to help them fade out of sight. Ceilings can be lowered for more intimacy. Room dividers can be used to create cozy corners, or block busy areas from general view. All this will help you to create a personality to your dining room that will compliment you *and* your customers, making you both happy to spend time there.

Your exterior design will have to accommodate the building you've selected and its architecture, naturally. Again, use soft, light colors wherever you can to attract attention. Your outside lighting will be particularly important, a factor that is often overlooked by the novice entrepreneur. Don't be afraid to put up a moderately large sign, if your local laws permit it, and to light it well enough so that it can be seen from a good distance down the road. Put your name on any canopy or awnings you use, especially over the front door. Without being garish, of course, let the world know you're there!

10

KITCHEN PLANNING

Wherever you place it in your overall plan, the kitchen will be the hub of all your activity, naturally. Sounds obvious, doesn't it? And of course it is. But how many times have you, personally, been in a restaurant recently where the space allotted to the preparation of food wasn't much larger than that given over to the jukebox? You're going to avoid that pitfall with your new restaurant.

In planning your floor space, then, *begin* with the kitchen area. You can locate it toward the back of the room, for best venting, between rooms for easy access, or even in the front window, if you or your chef feel you have the necessary flair and showmanship. For sheer advertising pulling-power, cooking in the window cannot be bettered.

Wherever you place it, your kitchen area *has* to be big enough and, above all, designed for maximum efficiency and ease in use under all conditions. That's really not as difficult to accomplish as it may sound if you will bear in mind—as you design the area—some rather simple but basic DO's and DON'Ts. Here are the main ones:

DOs

- Do design your kitchen so that one cook (or however many) can work with the least number of steps between major pieces of cooking equipment. This means that the cutting and preparations boards, lowboys, stove, refrigerator, freezer, deep-fryer, grill, sandwich board, and pass-through counter are all within as close a proximity to each other as is possible in your individual layout. If the refrigerator, for example, is at the far end of the room, your cooks will have to hustle down there each time they need something from it—always a time-waster. It will also break into their work flow, and ruin their concentration. Avoid that sort of thing with a little advance planning. For example, design the spaces to be occupied by your stove, deep-fryer, grill, and broiler as close to one another as you can—preferably alongside each other. This will allow you to utilize a single overhead hood and venting fan for all, and it will contain the heat, to a surprising degree, mainly in that one area.

- Do place your kitchen refrigerator(s) and freezer(s) side by side if at all possible, just outside but adjacent to the cooking area. Be sure the doors open from the most convenient side—they are built both ways.

- Do place your heavy shelving—those holding pots, pans, and other heavy utensils—overhead. You won't need to use these very often for storage, so it's pointless to allow them vital space. If possible, install pot racks up high, too.

- Shelving for dinner platters, however, must be nearest the pickup or pass-through counter. Many designs fail to allow space for this.
- Do allow *twice* as much flat-surfaced working area as you'd think you'd normally need. You'll never regret it.
- Do try to place your dishwashing area in fair proximity to your kitchen. In a small restaurant, not only can the dishwasher help in the prepping of food—meat cutting, shelling, and the like—he or she will inevitably also learn the rudiments of cooking from working so closely with the cooks. You will then have a live-in apprentice cook to fall back on in an emergency. It's also a splendid, All-American way to raise up a good worker both professionally and financially.
- In arranging the kitchen area into the blueprint of your restaurant, cut out little pieces of paper, in appropriate sizes, to represent the equipment you'll require. Use the list at the back of this book for your major pieces. Using your blueprint of the building (one big enough to show all wall indents and existing piping), move these little pieces of paper about to see just how things might possibly fit together. You will gain a good idea of the size of the equipment you'll need (and limitations) this way. And you will be astounded to realize just how many otherwise unseen combinations will present themselves. Besides, it sure beats pushing the stove around, doesn't it?
- Do spend the extra money and install rock tiles for the floors in your kitchen and dishwashing area.

The ease and security of keeping these floors clean and free from holes will more than repay the investment. And they will outlast even heavy industrial vinyl flooring by decades.

- Do keep the area well lighted, preferably with overhead, out-of-reach fluorescent tube lights of sufficient wattage. They can be had in pink hues for less glare and a more aesthetic appearance and still provide excellent illumination. Use a sliding plastic covering over any cooking-area lights. (In some localities this will be a health code requirement.) You have only to break a fluorescent bulb to realize why *this* precaution is needed. Bits of broken glass in your food is only really useful if the Borgias have asked you to cater their affair.

DON'Ts

- Don't divide your kitchen into two rooms.
- Don't cram all your kitchen equipment together so tightly that the cook(s) cannot move freely.
- Don't place all your equipment, on the other hand, so far apart from each other that your cooks will hit you up for roller skates.
- Never buy a stove with *less* than six jets. You'll need every one of them. With stoves, more *is* better.
- Don't separate freezers and refrigerators. Side by side is best. They are constant companions.
- Don't skimp on your grease filters or exhaust fan; a smoky restaurant will result, and that kind of smoke is *not* mysterious.

All these things are just common sense, really, but it's hard to remember everything, particularly if you're new to this fascinating restaurant business. Use the Dos and Don'ts as a checklist, and add to it on your own. But don't be put off if you find that you really cannot fit everything in as neatly as you would like. The perfect kitchen has often been designed, but has yet to be built.

Do the very best you can, be ingenious, and—above all —take all the *time* you need for the layout of your kitchen area. Once installed, it's sheer hell to alter. Then be content, knowing you've done as well as you (and your architect, if you have one) could do with the charms and limitations of the space.

Ummm. Can you smell those marvelous odors coming from your kitchen? Makes you hungry just thinking about it.

11

MENU DESIGN AND PRINTING

Your menu is, and always will be, your best advertising and selling tool. Let's make sure it really works for you.

I will assume—since you're already planning to open your own restaurant—that you have some sort of specific menu in mind. What I want to help you do here is to make that menu the very best possible of its kind.

There are currently in the book racks—usually in the larger-sized paperback format—three or four excellent compilations of menus from some of the nation's top or best-known restaurants. Such books are normally updated every year or so, so they are fairly reliable guides for all but pricing. Buy the lot, or as many as you can get, and look them over carefully. Each menu printed in these books is the product of hours and hours of concentrated labor, of trial and error, and—probably—hundreds of corrections, before it appears in the form you see.

It doesn't matter whether the particular restaurants whose menus appeal to you is the sort *you* contemplate opening. Study all the entrées, for example. Note, especially, the descriptions given. Note the variations in preparation, in sauces, in garnishes. And observe the number of ethnic treatments and Old World preparations for such otherwise mundane dishes as veal or chicken breast.

Make pencil notes of your own on a separate pad of all the foods, desserts, coffees, appetizers, or specialties that appeal to you or which you feel might be fitted into your own menu listing. Remember, you're probably going to need a fair number of daily specials in addition to your regular menu offerings. You'll be agreeably surprised, when you've done this selected copy-catting, at all the dishes you really had overlooked in your original concept.

When you take special notice of the entrée descriptions that appear on some of these menus, do they make you hungry just reading about them? Then go through and do likewise to thine own menu board.

Whatever format you choose, allow for *frequent* menu changes. Nothing is worse than an absolutely unvaried menu, especially to your good, steady customers. Even the fast food chains feature "specials," usually keyed to the seasons or holidays, but it's all by way of modifying their menus. Here are some of the ways you can effect changes in your own menu frequently without opening a printing shop of your own:

- Type up your menu daily, photocopy it, and insert it into book covers. You can photocopy onto a variety of colored papers, if you choose, varying the color each day.
- Allow space at the *top* of your menu for clip-ons (don't cover over anything if you can help it) that can announce daily specials or house recommen-

dations of the day. These are often handwritten and look very good that way if you have the time.

- In the larger cities there are menu printing firms who will print up a *portion* of your special daily or weekly menu onto your otherwise preprinted menu forms. This allows you latitude in entrées, mostly, with the balance of your board remaining the same.
- Provide a large blackboard menu, raised on high against a near wall for all to see. Or, you can choose half a dozen or so *portable* smaller blackboards on easels that your serving staff will bring to each table. This works best for tables only, since booth patrons on the inner side will be hard put to see properly.
- Hand-write your menus each day. Unless you love to write or print, however, this can become a distinct drag on a daily basis. You *could* photocopy, but, if so, be sure to use a dark, heavy-inked pen (or felt-tipped pen) for best results.
- Add menu "tents" on each table. This, however, more or less limits the number of daily temptations you can offer.

If your restaurant is in town, by all means place your menu in its own lighted box near the front door, or simply in the front window. Doing this assumes, of course, that your menu will sell for you, bringing potential (and hungry) customers right inside. To accomplish this feat you will have to design your menu, at least to a certain extent, like a colorful advertisement for your restaurant. Think back on all of the menus you've seen that really "sold" you. You'll probably find that they had these things in common:

- Manageable size and uncluttered format
- Large, easy-to-read type
- Savory and delectable descriptions of entrées
- Mixed price range
- Light, airy colors

Let's look at each of these dictums separately, to see how you might be able to apply them to your own menu format.

MANAGEABLE SIZE AND UNCLUTTERED FORMAT

Size and layout are almost equally important to you. Regardless of the quality of the food, an enormous, hundreds-of-choices menu is often an unwitting turnoff, as is the reverse—cute little booklets that take twenty minutes simply to read through. Moderation, as always, is the key word in your menu layout. In general, follow these considerations when designing your own menu:

- Leave a good margin and plenty of space between course entrées. If pinched for space, however, utilize boxes, circles, or any other appropriate enclosing design to separate areas.
- If you have an interesting logo, incorporate it into the menu design as an integral part.
- Choose an easy-to-hold size. *Standard* sizes will cost you considerably less, too, if your menu is to be printed.

- Allow blank space, if you can, *at top* for clip-ons of at least three by three inches. Try not to cover anything up.

LARGE, EASY-TO-READ TYPE

Sounds obvious, doesn't it? Yet how many times have you held a menu in your hands that you really couldn't read very well? Perhaps it was printed in brown type on tan menu paper that appeared to be perfectly readable in the office under the 150-watt overhead light there. When that menu got out onto the candle lamp–lit tables, however . . .

Remember, too, that a heavy part of the dining-out public these days is composed of senior citizens who no longer have to cook in for a growing family. Their eyesight—but, thank God, *not* their appetites!—ain't what it useta be. Make the type facing *dark, clear,* and *large.*

DELECTABLE DESCRIPTIONS OF ENTRÉES

While understatement certainly has no place on a menu, it's all too easy to go overboard on flowery entrée descriptions. Avoid that. Certainly your steak cuts should be named, set forth as "sizzling" or "broiled exactly to your order" or whatever, but don't call them "corn-fed" or "pampered" unless you know for a fact that they were. There's that Truth-in-Advertising Law on the books these days; your menu is, indeed, a prima facie advertising piece for your restaurant. If you plan to use fresh vegetables, be proud of the fact, and *say* "strictly fresh" on your menu. *Don't* say it if, as often as not, your vegetables will be frozen or fresh from the can. There are many appetizing ways to portray each of your entrées, desserts, appetizers, and specialties. Each description should help you sell the platter to your eager and hungry patrons. Be picturesque. But tell the truth, and keep all your expressions basically simple and, especially, believable.

MIXED PRICE RANGE

The rule here is not to be ignored: Vary your prices and your entrées as you list them, so that there is no steady progression, either up or down, in their costs. Mix your higher- and lower-cost dishes on your menu in no discernible order. This will ensure a more complete reading of all of your entrées by your budget-minded patrons.

LIGHT, AIRY COLORS

Above all, be practical in your choices of menu colors. While white type, for instance, on navy blue paper may *sound* attractive, in actuality it's dreadful. Again, simplicity pays dividends—the menu must be readable to everyone. Choose pastel shades—if not white itself—for your paper, and use black, fairly heavy, straightforward type. Your menu *covers*, on the other hand, can be any complementary color in the world, and help set the tone of your place from the start.

If you will be featuring your menu in your window, try to choose a color that will harmonize with both your inside *and* outside decor. Your menu, until your waiter or waitress arrives, is the prime selling tool for your entire restaurant.

Finally, write out your menu as clearly as you can. If entrées are "à la carte," say so, in large print. If you offer a choice of appetizer *or* soup *or* dessert, print it up just the way I did, to avoid misleading or annoying any of your patrons. If there's to be an additional charge for anything —rolls and butter, for example—make no secret of that fact on your menu. Your customers must be able to understand it all on just one reading.

Try to avoid, if at all possible, that most hideous and downright unfriendly of menu warnings: No substitutions. Why *not*, f'gosh sakes? *Give* them a salad instead of potato, and *help* them keep on their diets. Accommodate them, and they'll be taking seats in your place a lot more often. Making friends for yourself is awfully easy if you avoid any semblance of boarding-school finger waving.

12

CONTRACTORS

Contractors are, unfortunately, an essential headache. Unless you are a master electrician, plumber, and builder, you cannot create your new restaurant without them. So take two aspirins, and let's look into this area with the view to avoiding as many pitfalls as we can.

If your budget can possibly manage it, hire an architect/engineer as a first step in actually planning the reality of your new place. Not only will this professional be able to make accurate renderings for you in proper scale, so you will be able to visualize what your ideas will *really* look like, but he can probably advise you beforehand just how adaptable to practicality those ideas are. You wanted a walk-in refrigerator *there?* Better not, since drainage there is difficult, and it's too close to the furnace, anyway. Architects are skilled in all such areas, and can set your plans up for you in the most efficient way after inspecting the place or your site. He knows from experience just what will work and what will probably not work. If your architect is something of an engineer as well (and most of the restaurant architects are), he'll be

able to advise you on plumbing and electrical requirements and standards, including securing the permits and
inspections you'll need in your locality. In addition, he is
often in a position to recommend a general contractor to
you, one he's worked with before and knows; since it's his
reputation and responsibility, then, as well as yours, he'll
be a valuable ally whenever contractual problems arise.

Don't be at all hesitant to seek out an architect. Architects are in business to help *you* bring *your* ideas into
realization. Competent architects will *not* try to impose
upon you any of their ideas unless you ask for them, nor
will they suggest any damn-the-expense methods for accomplishing any task. On the contrary, they will more
than pay for their hiring by *saving* you money—by avoiding built-in problem areas, with suggestions for solutions
you alone may never have thought of. They are knowledgeable in the very areas in which you'll probably be
needing the most help. Talk with several architects, if
you can. But hire one of them as a *first step* in the creation
of your own business. You'll never regret it.

Should you, however, have to hire contractors strictly
on your own, then first make out a *thorough* listing of all
the work that has to be done by each. You will be far
better able to talk intelligently with your carpenter, electrician, plumber, and heating contractors if you know—
and *they* know you know—precisely what each one is
being asked to do for you. Quotations for the work will be
closer to the final truth, as well, if you can present each
contractor with a comprehensive list of the tasks to be
commissioned.

Take your time in compiling these lists, and try to
make them as all-inclusive as you know how. Better to

overreach than to underestimate. Then attempt to get these items incorporated into the contractual agreements you and your contractors will draw up and sign before any actual work commences. The listing at the back of this book can serve as a starting guide for you here.

Also try to get some actual *dates* into your contracts, both for starting and for completion, as best you can, so that overtime costs are held to a minimum for all of you.

Be prepared to give all of your contractors some percentage of their money due before they start (usually enough to allow them to buy the raw materials they'll need for the job), with the balance doled out, by previous agreement *on paper*, as the work progresses. Make sure your attorney looks over any contracts you make *before* you sign them, in order to put in provisions for postponed payments in case of work stoppage, a strike, or delays above and beyond reasonable expectations.

There probably *will* be delays all along the line in getting all contractual work completed. It's inevitable, somehow. Stalled delivery of needed materials is very often a reason given, and most of the time it is probably true. Discuss this aspect with your contractors in advance, to determine if they anticipate *any* difficulties with any parts or materials called for. If so, try to agree upon some substitutes rather than experience a slowdown or work stoppage once the actual work has begun. Most contractors know what materials are in short supply, and will be delighted to see that *you* realize this, too. You'll save a bundle this way, since everybody works more efficiently when uninterrupted.

If Contractors A, B, and C all give you bids that are not substantially far apart from each other on costs, but Contractor D comes in with a quotation that's much, *much* lower—*beware* of Contractor D. Either he'll be adding costs later for "unforeseeable" reasons, or he'll recoup the difference by buying cheaper parts (for which you'll pay and pay later) or he's planning on using nonunion, perhaps substandard, help on your job. In the latter case you may not be able to pass local inspections, since most states require much of the work be done only by *licensed* contractors.

I know of one instance when a new restaurateur hired a nonlicensed "midnight electrician" whose bid came in at exactly half that of any of the others, presumably because he would be doing the work on his own after the usual work hours. When it was discovered that he was not licensed—even though the work seemed to be in good order—no inspector could be secured to come and approve the installations. Finally a licensed man had to be brought in. All the previous work was torn out, since the new electrician had no other way of assuring himself that the materials and workmanship were, in fact, correct. The end result was, of course, one and a half times as expensive, with a delay of two weeks added before opening.

Be on hand as often as you can manage when your contractual work is actually being done. Without making a pest of yourself, of course, ask each worker to tell you what he is working on that very minute and what, if any, problems he is encountering. Surprisingly, the workers will not resent you, as long as you don't intrude too often and you demonstrate a knowledgeable and lively interest in what they're accomplishing for you.

But don't, f'gosh sakes, ever *advise*. If you sense that

something is not right, take it up immediately with the foreman or the head contractor, but never the individual worker on the spot.

And when warranted, give some compliments to the people doing the work—we *all* appreciate that, don't we?

13

SAFETY EQUIPMENT

At various times in this handbook I have touched on security, and fire-prevention systems. This area is so important—and so often overlooked in the first planning of a new restaurant—that it deserves special attention here in its own chapter.

FIRE PROTECTION

Let's take a look at fire-prevention systems first. In most localities a built-in system—consisting of one or more tanks of a dry extinguishing chemical and a series of overhead nozzles—*must*, by fire code laws, be installed. The system is placed directly over your stove, deep-fryer, grill, and other actual cooking areas. In the event of a blaze in any of these areas, the chemical is automatically released, putting out the fire before it has had a chance to grow and prosper. The best known right now are the Ansul or Kidde systems, which work on fundamentally the same layouts.

It's possible to secure a rebuilt fire-prevention system, and it will save you about one-half the cost of a new one.

But be certain, if you do, that it conforms with the *latest* requirements in your community. Such requirements are updated regularly, usually becoming more stringent and encompassing each time. Check with your fire department, inspection division, or the Health Department.

A brand-new fire-prevention system will come with warranties, but it's a wise precaution to have your local extinguisher-protection people (look in the Yellow Pages under "Fire Protection") check your system, whatever the age, at least twice a year. A certificate of such inspections may be a fire department requirement, but even if it's not, such inspections on a regular basis will, in all probability, help you reduce the cost of your fire insurance.

Since most restaurant fires start in the cooking area, this requirement only makes good sense. What greater protection for your new restaurant, after all, than a system that will go into action *automatically* when needed? Machines never panic.

You will also need a quantity of hand-held fire extinguishers placed strategically around the entire restaurant, kitchen, storage, and compressor rooms. At least two must be in or near the kitchen itself, but *not* mounted next to the stove or deep-fryer. Mount another near the top of any stairway, with another at the bottom. Keep at least one in the compressor area, one in the storage room, and one or two extras in your office. They, too, should be checked out when your kitchen system is inspected. Be sure they are all of the ABC formula, which will put out *all* types of flames from simple cigarette burns to grease fires.

As we have said elsewhere, make sure you ask your

electrician to provide you with automatic cutoffs on your compressor motors. These will shut the motors down in case your compressors should get too hot for any reason, and thus prevent any of them from burning up. It's a simple precaution—again, often overlooked somehow— and inexpensive to install. Do it.

SMOKE-DETECTION SYSTEM

You most certainly ought to consider the placement of a smoke-detection system in your dining room, kitchen, and compressor and storage rooms. Use a system that can be switched off during the day when your restaurant is occupied, since cigarette and cooking smoke combined would trigger the alarm. Put it on full operation at night, after closing, and anytime the restaurant is closed. If possible, get it connected with the police and fire department phones. Some states may require this by law.

SECURITY

A security system will protect you from burglary when you're closed, and from a holdup (sometimes) when you're all on hand. A silent alarm can be installed behind your bar or near the cashier, which will ring in the police precinct but not in the restaurant. It's dangerous to use, however, since those who attempt a holdup, wielding weapons, are as frightened as you are, and just might lose their heads if they see you doing something like pressing a button. Best bet is to put away (or deposit) all large bills as the day progresses, as often as necessary. Then the thieves will get *something* for their effort (they won't stop to count it, y'know) and leave as quickly as they came. It's a frightening thought either way.

Certainly an overnight burglary security system is recommended for *all* restaurants in urban areas, with your needs here otherwise tailored to your individual community. Obviously, if you build on a three-by-five-mile ocean island usually encased in fog you won't need one at all!

In general, it's a good idea to protect what you've built as best as your budget will allow. There are many systems on the market, from simple door or window alarms all the way to tape or pressure systems that encircle your entire restaurant when you're not there. Check these out locally, since prices vary a good deal even for the same kind of protection. Most taping is charged by leasing the service on a monthly basis, after the installation cost is met, which means you can spread the cost out all year.

Some systems will have a police department or security guard hookup that will automatically call them (*and* you!) in the event of an after-hours burglary. While such a call system can go haywire occasionally, or be falsely set off at closing time (with the resultant automatic telephone call to you at three A.M.), it's a generally unbeatable system, and I highly recommend it.

14

FOOD PURCHASING

This is one of our shortest chapters because the problem of purchasing food and liquor is, probably, the easiest to solve. To the novice entrepeneur, this aspect seems enormous, I know. But it really isn't. Unless you're planning to open your new restaurant on an out-island of the Hebrides, your purveyors will—with astonishing speed—find *you*.

However, you cannot allow yourself to be satisfied just to sit back and interview the salespeople as they pour in. Get out from behind your desk and *go see* what your prospective wholesalers' places of business really look like. Are they clean? Do the butchers insist you wear a white jacket and a hat? (They should.) Are there any rotting foodstuffs around on the floors? Do they welcome your visit, or are they "too busy" to see you?

You may not be able to do this with liquor wholesalers, but they present no health problems to you. However, it's worthwhile to visit your local produce wholesalers, bakers, butchers, and butter-egg-and-cheese purveyors at least once. Get to know the voices at the other end of your telephone when you call in your orders. Nothing works better in *any* business than the personal touch. And then you'll have a person you know to compliment or complain to as the occasion arises.

By all means select and systematically buy from *more than one* wholesale purveyor in each category of your needs. Always do business with at least two butchers, two produce wholesalers, and two bakers, as far as it is feasible. Make it a rule to be "in" to new salespeople who will attempt to sell you a better or less expensive grade (or both!) of coffee or glassware, or heads of lettuce. Listen to them. Try out any samples they give you. Ask others on your staff—or even good customers—to join you in a taster's round, and to tell you, frankly, what they think of the product. Not only will this be enjoyable for all of you, but you will, inevitably, discover some better products or easier prices this way.

Naturally, you will comparison shop as you go along. Many times—most times, in fact—case loads will be considerably cheaper for you to buy than small quantities. Beer and wine distributors frequently will give you an extra case for each dozen or so purchased at one time, for example. If you can afford it, buy this way, and simply store the overflow until you need it.

Quality usually extracts its just price. You will have to be the judge on all of this, pitting top quality, sometimes, against your budget and available funds. Do not, however, go to extremes, buying *only* the finest, the most expensive, unless you plan your entrée prices to match. "Fine quality at a low price" doesn't exist these days, and it's doubtful if it *ever* did.

Done properly and with care, the selection of your purveyors should be a rewarding experience, and not a drag at all. Sipping wines, sampling steaks, trying out beautiful, gloriously fattening desserts—I mean, can that really be a tough way to make a living?

15

MENU PRICING AND QUALITY CONTROLS

One of the reasons I suggested you keep your own ledgers and books on a daily or weekly basis is simply that this is a prime method of keeping in constant touch with the daily costs and charges of your services and food. With prices seemingly ever upward, alert restaurateurs will have to rewrite the prices on their basic menus *three or four times per year* in order to maintain the same margin of real profit.

You, too, must be prepared to make these price revisions, or suffer the fate of many restaurants-in-trouble: while their income remains the same, higher operating costs each month causes their net to be reduced proportionately. You can't afford—literally—to be lazy for a moment. After all, what's the point in troubling to open a good restaurant at all unless you intend to make an excellent living at it all year round?

PRICING

Well, then, what do you really have to charge in order to make a profit? There is, in this business, a general Rule of Three, which applies not only to total salaries (not more than one-third your gross) but equally to pricing. Simply stated, this is it: The amount you charge for a complete meal, or entrée, must be *at least three times the total cost* to you for all its ingredients.

Just exactly *what* does that mean in down-to-earth serving terms? Let's take as an example a complete sirloin steak dinner entrée, which will consist of the cut of steak itself, a baked potato, a fresh vegetable, a salad and its dressing, with fresh rolls and butter.

For our illustration of the Rule of Three, let us now assume that one pound of sirloin, delivered but untrimmed, will come to five dollars, wholesale. Cutting the meat, paring away excess fat, and shaping it into eight-ounce steaks ready for your broiler will waste about 20 percent—so the cost of one pound, really, is now six dollars. Each eight-ounce steak, then, costs you three dollars.

There is no waste at all in a baked potato. It's cost will remain as delivered. Let's assume it's about 20 cents, with butter or sour cream adding another 10 cents. Vegetables vary according to season, naturally, so you'll probably choose one that's plentiful—and inexpensive—in the markets at the time. Whichever you select, the vegetables will have to be sliced or trimmed, so we can calculate about 25 percent above the basic cost of a serving. Let's assume it's broccoli, and you plan to serve approximately three good spears. Taking into account your waste on this, we might figure the cost per serving, with a sauce, at about 40 cents.

Salad, consisting of mixed greens, will add about 15 cents, the dressing 10 cents; rolls and butter (average consumption per person) should come in no higher than 30 cents. That's our entrée, and a nice one it is. Getting hungry?

Now to figure what to charge. The total cost to you of all the ingredients in our entrée comes to $4.25. Multiply this figure by *three*. Your menu price, then, should be no lower than $12.75. This price will automatically take into account all your other expenses, proportionately—rent, heat, salaries, insurance, utilities, and so on—in order to assure you a *net* profit from that meal of about 10 to 15 percent (or from $1.27 to $1.91), depending on your own variables.

Of course, if your basic rent is low, or you own your building and the taxes are reasonable (Fantasyland), your net profit will be higher. If the neighborhood warrants it—Wall Street, for instance—you can reasonably charge $18.95 for that same entrée. Do it, by all means. Pricing often comes down, really, to considering *just what the traffic will bear.*

The Rule of Three is *not* exact, and is not intended to be. It's meant to serve you as a guide, a starting point, if you will, to help you in your entrée pricing. You must also take into consideration any unusul expenses—a percentage of your gross taken as part of your rent, for example, or unusually high rent. I know of a pleasant restaurant located in a reconverted ferry boat; here the proprietor has to add a percentage to his prices for *docking*!

Your competitor's prices will have to be considered, probably. However, you can usually vary *your* pricing about 10 percent without suffering any qualms about your patrons' pocketbooks.

If your food is downright *superb*, or your hot dogs a foot

and a half long, *then*, by George, you're in a league by yourself, and you can charge whatever you want. You'll get it.

QUALITY CONTROLS

Quality controls are as important to the success of your new business as inventory controls. Being a restaurateur, you are Mom in the Kitchen, subliminally, to many of your steadiest customers. Like Mom, you will want to keep them healthy as well as fully fed. Whatever you serve, be it prime ribs to pancakes, give your customers the very *best* you can afford. Often it's the little things that matter most. Never foist wilted lettuce on your patrons—better to be out entirely, substituting a vegetable, slaw, applesauce, or sherbet instead. Stale rolls set a bad mood for the whole meal, as does tepid or anemic soup.

The best method of controlling quality is to run the kitchen yourself. Next best is to dine at your own restaurant often, but *never* let the cooks know the order they're filling is for you. Vary your tastes, so no pattern or habit is ever set. ("Don't worry about that burned bacon, Pierre —the boss *never* orders it.") Read the riot act to any chef who tries to palm off overdone or badly cooked meats or vegetables. If the problem is built in, you may have to make some kitchen changes, or add more equipment. If not, you might have to look for another cook. But, once set, *never* allow your standards to sink. You'll lose even your friendliest patrons, never to see them again. Besides, *you* eat there, too.

NUTRITION

Hand in hand with good quality control is good nutrition. Try to give your customers as *balanced* a meal as

possible for their *own* good as well as yours. Don't skimp
on vegetables or eliminate them entirely. Prepare a salad
that *looks* as good as it is good for you. Don't slice your
tomatoes so thin you can read a newspaper through them.
Really *care* what your patrons and friends are served in
your establishment.

Too much food, of course, is as bad as too little, and an
enormous waste as well. If you must overdo (all your
patrons are lumberjacks), err on the side of foods that
are plentiful and relatively cheap to prepare—spaghetti,
French-fried potatoes, copious salads, an extra slice of
bacon, or endless coffee. The latter, if you can afford to
do it, is always recommended. Bountiful fresh coffee,
usually coming at the end of a meal (and served with a
smile), will inevitably result in greater satisfaction, and
better tips.

Which brings us to leftovers. What'll you *do* with leftovers? Surprisingly, very little food is wasted in the average good restaurant, partly due to intelligent buying patterns, based on a knowledge of patrons' preferences. Most
restaurants, in addition, will simply refrigerate most leftover soups, uncooked vegetables, sauces, and specialty
dishes just as you would in your own kitchen at home.
Breads, rolls, and many desserts can be placed in the
freezer without any harm. Hamburger meat that will not
store another day can be immediately cooked into meat-
loaf, meat balls, ethnic specialties, and other baked de-
lights, and *then* refrigerated.

Your most expensive shellfish will be kept frozen, then
refrigerated, until ordered. Steaks are cut daily, in antici-
pation of a calculated number of sales; if fresh when delivered, any excess can be frozen at the end of the day. Your
"specials of the day" should be prepared in limited quan-

tities, so you will probably run out before closing. And so it goes. Any foods that sour, or turn, *must* be thrown out immediately, of course. But a good cook will keep the likelihood of this down to an absolute minimum. After all, everyone hates to waste food.

16

THAT ALL-IMPORTANT OFFICE

Since running a restaurant is akin to being in show business, you'll need—like a popular actor—a quiet room in which to get away from the public from time to time. You can't be "on stage" all the time, nor should you be expected to be. However, the only place in the entire establishment to which a restaurateur can retire, really, is his office.

That's reason enough, by itself, for creating a comfortable office area. If space permits—and your hideaway office can be *anywhere*—try to furnish it with an easy chair or two, perhaps even a divan, if possible. You'll be able, then, to utilize your office for small meetings or conferences when you do *not* want to be disturbed. And, with a couch, you will be able to grab a catnap now and again when business is slow—one of the unique privileges of proprietorship!

Offices, however, no matter how comfortably furnished, also mean business. You'll need an average-size desk with in and out boxes and overhead shelving, a filing cabinet (legal width), a flexible lamp, a telephone, bookshelves, and a computer-type adding machine with tape attach-ment.

Most offices seem to lack a workable amount of simple, flat surfaces on which to put papers and files. Try using two double-drawer filing cabinets in place of one four-drawer cabinet. This will allow you *two* very usable flat-top surfaces at a height that will easily accommodate your telephone, adding machine, and all the other bits and snags of paper that need to be seen and attended to. If your budget is pinched, lay a smooth-faced interior door over these cabinets and—presto!—you have created a sev-en-foot-long desk.

Build in as many shelves as you can. Install them over your desk, on the side walls, everywhere—you'll need every one.

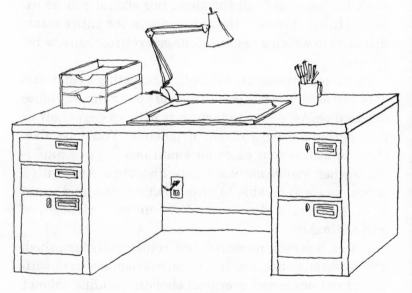

A door desk.

And don't forget to allow a spot atop your desk for photographs of the special people in your life, to remind yourself why you're doing all this!

You'll be required by law to keep these records at hand in your office:

- Approved Building Department plans and blueprints of all floors.
- Copies of all permits and licenses (including liquor).
- Daily wage and hour records for all your employees.
- Copies of your insurance policies. Put the originals in your safety deposit box.
- Records of all federal, state, and local taxes paid.
- A ledger detailing daily gross income figures and expenses paid.
- Copies of all leases, ownership, and mortgage papers.

In addition, you should keep these records in your office, too:

- A bills-pending (unpaid) folder, alphabetized for easy access.
- Bank statements and canceled checks, filed together by the month.
- All paid bills, dated when paid with check number, and filed away under the *individual* purveyor's name.
- Your checkbook (hide this, or lock it up when not in use).

Your payroll records must be kept up to date, since they are accountable at any time for state or federal audit. (This doesn't happen very often, but it's best to be prepared.) You'll certainly need them completed every three months for your state and federal quarterly reports. (These are forms that list each employee's individual wages, and withholdings, for a three-month period, and must be filed every quarter.) They are automatically mailed to your each quarter.

This is also a good time to calculate your own payroll expenses in light of a three month's revenue income. Your total payroll should not exceed approximately one-third of your gross. This will include or exclude your own salary, depending entirely on the amount of work you, personally, put in to earn it. It is a rule of thumb, of course, and is meant to be more a guide to you than a fixed and fast rule.

However, if your total payroll is substantially higher—40 to 45 percent, for example—you are *probably* headed for trouble. Examine your salary structures, as well as the number of staff you employ each work period, and try to make some cuts. You might find that you have more people working for you than you really need. If you cannot manage to do that, then reexamine your menu prices, upping them to bring in more money per entrée. Do *both*. Discuss your payroll problems frankly with a good accountant, who may be able to suggest some tax breaks in your situation.

Don't delay. Most restaurants slide into financial trouble not because of any lack of patrons, but because their expenses are higher than anticipated. Since salaries constitute the single largest expenditure you have, look there, first, for some practical relief.

If you employ an accountant on a retainer basis, he will supply you with the necessary ledgers and payroll books you'll need. Even so, it's essential—particularly for the first year—to make all the entries in both of these books *yourself*, leaving your accountant the job of summing up each quarter. There is no better way for you to actually *see* how your money is spent, what it buys, and who gets it. You'll learn your peak and your dead hours of business. You'll be able, after a short while, to approximate the revenue generated by your kitchen at breakfast, lunch, and dinner on each of the days you're open. You will be able to determine how well your bar is faring for you, and when *its* peaks are likely to occur. No amount of graphs or charts prepared by professionals will ever take the place of this personal bookkeeping.

A daily report—per shift—is highly recommended for all but the smallest restaurants. On it can be recorded the cash register tape totals as well as the totals of all your guest checks. (Let's hope they balance within a dollar or two!) Any pertinent information having to do with the shift's performance that day can also be noted. For example, if you had a blizzard last Thursday, *that* was probably the reason your gross was way below average for most Thursdays. Keep these records—a month or two from now you'll never remember the exact date of that blizzard. And you can use these daily reports in compiling your official books as long as each shows your bankable gross for the day.

At right is a sample of a very simple daily shift report. Make up your own to fit your basic information needs. Photocopy a couple hundred, at least, at a time.

YE OLDE SNAGGLETOOTH CAFE

Day: *Monday*   Shift: *A.M.*

Date: *1/8/88*   Manager: *Zelda*

Total Cash and Charge Cards, attached: *$690.00*

Register tape total *$810.80*

Guest check total *810.00*

Payouts, if any (receipts) *20.00*

Difference, if any (*) *.80*

Starting cash box *200.00*

Ending cash box *300.00*

Difference, if any (**) *100.00*

Remarks: *Refused 2 cases of lettuce from ABC — bottom rows not fresh. Note statement.*

(*) Explanation: *80¢ error in ringing up. See marked tape.*

(**) Explanation: *Upped cash box $100. — for P.M. use.*

In our example, the first line (*actual* cash money plus any credit card receipts for the entire shift) is $120.80 *less* than the register tape. Why? Three reasons, all of which are explained in detail on the daily shift report sheet. The biggest difference, $100, occurred by beefing up the starting cash box (which contains small bills and rolls of coins for change) for the night shift, which is expected to be busier. There was a $20 payout, in cash, during that shift; the receipt attached to the report explained *that*. And an 80-cent error in handling the cash register during the period accounts for the balance. This error was found, marked on the tape, and the tape itself attached to the report as well. The report, while extremely simple, is complete with all its attachments, including the guest checks used.

In our example, the starting cash box will probably be *reduced* by the night shift manager at the end of *its* duty period, resulting in a $100 overage for that shift. This, too, will be recorded on the daily shift report.

The sum totals of both the A.M. and the P.M. reports will make up your entire day's gross. From this you can figure your sales tax manually, or you can use your cash register tape if you rang up the tax separately.

Enter the total gross and taxes into your company books directly from these reports. After that, you can elect to keep them or not, since they are not official forms. Generally, it's best to file them for about a year, since the information on them—especially under Remarks—might be useful in establishing sales *patterns* by days of the weeks and months of the year. Such patterns are particularly useful should you ever wish to sell your restaurant.

Any other income, such as cigar and cigarette sales,

insurance refunds, and the like, should be entered separately in your ledger. They have their own taxes or, in the case of the refund, none at all, so never list this income with your regular daily gross totals.

For payments that *you* make, enter each check and its number on appropriate pages of your monthly books under Expenses Incurred. Do the same for any cash payouts. Your books must show you exactly *where* every penny spent went. If, for example, you write three checks, one for the butcher, one to the telephone company, and the last in favor of your laundry supply firm, you will list each under its *own* heading on the Expenditures pages of your monthly books. In our example, the butcher's paid bill would be entered in the column headed Food Suppliers, the telephone check would be noted under Utilities, and the laundry payment could probably be entered under Supplies or Services. You can make up your own headings, or use an accountant's preprinted forms. It will all come out the same, however you do it.

These are all *your* records. They are, in a way, the story of your restaurant's rise to fame and success. As such, they are extremely important to you. Keeping them up on a daily basis is usually not necessary, as long as you have your daily shift reports on hand. But a weekly or, certainly, monthly updating is critical, in order to total the income figures on which you will pay monthly sales taxes, federal deposits, and Social Security payments.

But most of all your books will tell you just how well you're *really* doing, since all your income and all your expenses are reflected together there for the first time. And should you ever wish to sell (at an *enormous* profit, naturally), you'll need these same books to make up the P and Ls (profit and loss) figures for each year.

In your office, then, one more important piece of equipment had better be set up—a good, substantial pencil sharpener.

17

INSURANCE

All dreams must, sooner or later, come face to face with reality, and this is particularly true in the restaurant field. Without dreams you will not create anything. But even as you begin to build upon your dreams, you must take steps to protect them, to *insure*, as it were, that they will come true.

For that reason, protection, in the form of insurance, should be seen to before the first carpenter cuts a single board in your new restaurant. Either through the services of a broker, or directly, secure a blanket liability policy that will protect you *and* all the workers you'll have to use. *Don't begin work without one.* Do we really have to elaborate on the possible consequences of *not* bothering?

You should find it possible, at the same time, to secure some limited fire coverage during this construction period. It, too, will be well worth the relatively small cost, since neither of these policies—assuming the standard limitations—is prohibitively expensive.

Once you complete construction to the point that you

can begin to hire permanent restaurant help, you'll need to consider the following insurance:

- Workmen's compensation
- Fire (casualty)
- "Umbrella" coverage
- Burglary/robbery/vandalism
- Increased liability
- Health and retirement
- Business interruption

Let's take a brief look at each of these in turn, so you can gain a fair idea of your own needs and be able to talk with your insurance agent on a one-to-one basis.

WORKMEN'S COMPENSATION

Here you really have no options, since this insurance is mandated. You *have* to have it, by law. Rates are also set by law—a good thing, actually, since this insurance would undoubtedly be considerably more expensive if it weren't.

Workmen's compensation insurance protects all the employees on your payroll against accidents and mishaps endured while working on your premises. It also protects *you* if you set up a corporation. When an employee of yours sustains a burn, a cut, or even broken bones—such things do happen in the food service field—compensation and hospital care are provided for with this policy.

A word to the new entrepreneur: If you hire some employees to work for you in any capacity *off* the payroll books, be aware that you and they are *not* covered by workmen's compensation insurance in the event of an accident. If you're sued, you're on your own, and heaven help you. It isn't worth the risk.

FIRE (CASUALTY)

An insurance company representative will visit your new premises, inspect it, and rate it as a fire risk on a scale from one to ten, one being the best. The representative will take into consideration such things as the type of building (wooden is not the best), the actual experience of management, the wiring and plumbing, the placement of fire extinguishers and overhead protective fire equipment, and the number of exits.

Depending on your rating, this insurance will or will not be expensive. It's also fairly hard to get these days, many insurance organizations having decided to drop restaurant coverage entirely. Regardless, plug on. You *must* have fire insurance, and it can be obtained, frequently, by securing coverage from more than one carrier, each insuring a portion of the whole.

UMBRELLA COVERAGE

An insurance broker can be of inestimable help in securing proper coverage in most cases. By placing all of your insurance with one or two carriers, a broker can sometimes garner policies for you that you, alone, would be hard put to duplicate. In fact, as a new restaurateur you would be well advised to seek out the services of a local insurance broker as soon as you sign on the dotted line for your new place. A broker who has written all, or most, of your business may be able, for example, to acquire a good umbrella policy for you, covering liability, fire, theft, and other areas, in amounts of coverage (a million dollars or more!) that will *really* protect you and your neighbors from even the worst happenstances. In addition, your broker should be able to advise you on all your needs as time goes by and your restaurant grows. And this same person will go to bat for you with the insurance companies when and if you ever need it.

A smoke-detection system is not necessarily required in insurance policies, to date, but it make *great* sense—and will help your own peace of mind, incidentally—to install some. Put them in the restaurant proper, as well as in the compressor room and kitchen.

BURGLARY/ROBBERY/VANDALISM

The amount of coverage you'll need here depends primarily on the size and scope of your business. At the very least, however, secure holdup (robbery) coverage, which usually also indemnifies you or any of your employees en route to the bank on regular or night deposit visits.

Whether you'll really need either burglary (breaking in when your place is closed) or vandalism insurance depends mostly on your neighborhood. You already know the answers here. Again, the amount of coverage should be no more than the replacement value of the most likely items to be stolen or wrecked. No one, for instance, is *ever* going to carry away your two hundred-pound stainless-steel mixer or cast-iron stoves.

INCREASED LIABILITY

Once you're ready to open your doors to the swarming public, you'll have to consider increasing your liability insurance coverages to indemnify these categories:

- Product liability. This will protect you in case of food poisonings, contamination, broken glassware, and all such horrors.
- Staff. You'll need some protection beyond workmen's compensation in the case of a suit or negligence claims against you by an employee.
- Customer protection. You'll be surprised how often your patrons will fall down, manage to get cut, or generally outraged at something or other. Then there's the age-old "I found a piece of metal in my tuna fish sandwich!" gambit to be contended with. You must be protected here as well.
- Liquor liability. In some states the proprietor who maintains a bar or serves liquor, beer, or wine is somehow responsible for the condition of his customers even after they've left the restaurant. Ridiculous, but true, nonetheless. Check out *your* local laws in this regard, and cover yourself accordingly.

HEALTH AND RETIREMENT

Eventually you'll have to come to grips with these problems. The most important at this stage of your business is some kind of health and hospital coverage for both you and your staff. Blue Cross is probably the largest and best known of the insurers in this area these days, but your broker or insurance representative may have other suggestions. Be cautious. *Read* every paragraph so you'll know what each type of policy will actually offer you. Make notes as you read. Medical policies vary enormously. Note especially the "deductible" amounts required.

If you are dealing with a union, such a policy *will* be a requirement. The union may even be able to help you here. You can offer to pay it all (and you must cover the employee himself) or part of it, depending on the number of dependents each employee wants also covered.

BUSINESS INTERRUPTION

We come, finally, to a policy you really *don't* have to have. Business interruption will cover you, the owner, and perhaps a few key employees, in the event of a disaster to your restaurant that would require you to close down for major repairs of a fair period of time.

Generally speaking, unless you can get this kind of coverage written into an umbrella policy, business interruption insurance is both very expensive and, hopefully, unnecessary. If your new restaurant is located within the shadow of an active volcano, buy it.

You should now be covered pretty thoroughly by insurance. You're almost ready to open those doors . . .

18

FURTHER PAPER WORK— WHAT TO EXPECT

Before your contractor can begin any structural work such as adding walls, major flooring repairs, or setting up a kitchen area for you, he must have architectural plans (blue prints) to do the work properly. In most communities these must be drawn up and submitted to the local Buildings Department for inspection and approval. Your architect—or even your contractor—can usually do this for you.

Once you have your floor plans approved, make *several* copies of them right away. Keep a good half dozen on file in your office during your building period. The fire department, your insurance agent, the Board of Health (and several other municipal departments you've never known existed before) will *all* require a complete set before they will be able to issue you the proper permits to operate your new restaurant. You'll save *days* in time, and a good deal in frustration, if you already have copies on hand to give the inspectors.

In addition, keep office files for copies (put the originals in a safety deposit box, please) of your lease, your mortgage papers, and any other building-connected contracts, so you'll always be able to find them for reference when needed. These are the basics.

Our federal government prints many booklets to aid the small-business man. That's *you*, probably. One of the best, and highly recommended, is a small book that will guide you in the understanding and preparation of all the federal tax forms that will apply once you're open—and some that will apply even before that date. Ask for it at your Internal Revenue office. Most of these books and phamplets are usually available to you there, either free, or at a nominal cost. Do this even if you have engaged a regular accountant.

You'll need to know your local and state regulations on employing minors. You'll probably employ some sooner or later. Wages and hours for them are spelled out in bulletins issued by each state, as are the appropriate "working papers" needed if an employee of yours is still in high school. Their schools will supply these papers for you to sign. You must have them, and keep them in your office on file.

Women come under certain employment regulations that differ from those covering men, regarding such things as dressing rooms, and personal security. All such recommendations and procedures, most of which are just common sense, will be covered in the same bulletin.

All discrimination, naturally, is prohibited, as well it ought to be. This injunction extends beyond matters of race, religion, and color these days to include a balance, as much as possible, between male and female employees. Unless your operation is to be quite small, or unsuited to one sex or the other, you must try to hire both. *You* might enjoy that better, too—and it frequently makes for greater harmony, a better "family" feeling, all around.

Unions, usually, are more concerned with the larger operations such as resorts, large diners, hotels, and popular restaurant chains. Your staff may or may not be approached. Some communities are far more unionized in general than others. Try to ascertain this *before* you settle on a location by checking around at your already established would-be competitors. Judge, if you can, how efficiently a union house appears to be running. Take note of the sunny or sour disposition of most of the union help. Are the waiters and waitresses slovenly or neat? Attentive or bored? Cooperative, or standoffish? Is the same more or less true of *all* the restaurants in that area? If you come up with only negatives, move on. It's an indication that the local unions are, in all probability, a bit too powerful in that community.

On the other hand, put yourself in the place of one of your own employees for a moment. What do you need, now, above and beyond your basic salary, to keep your working life relatively happy and productive? Certainly a comprehensive health insurance program *must* be offered to everyone, regardless of position, after a trial period of six weeks or so. A schedule that allows for overtime pay for all consecutive hours over eight per day should be a house rule. Compensation for working on holidays should be instituted. Sick days should be provided, to a point. Parking spaces available to your help, and clean dressing rooms (with lockers that *lock*) will go a long, long way in keeping your personnel content, obviously.

If you can offer them as many benefits as a union can,

your staff will probably reject any unionization attempt. Where there's no gripe, there's no need to pay union dues, is there?

Ours is a bureaucratic form of government. Be prepared, therefore, to secure, put up, frame, and file all manner of local and state permits. The restaurant field is one of the most regulated in the world. Each inspection is usually preceded by an official form mailed to you requesting information (and, of course, a check) by such diverse bureaus covering buildings, health, highways, fire, boilers, liquor, utility, awnings, historical compliance, outside signs, lighting, and consumer affairs. And two or three more "bureaus" that boggle the mind. New York City, for example, even has a place-of-assembly permit—whatever else *is* a restaurant?

No matter. Sooner or later you'll have an entire wall papered with permits, and you'll be able at last to get down to the serious business of serving good food, and enjoying life.

19

HEALTH
INSPECTION

It is my aim in this chapter to provide you with my recommendations—and in some areas, *mandates*—for the construction of the kitchen of your new restaurant. If you follow this advice carefully, your health inspector will be delighted with your new place. He may even eat there *himself*.

Your first step is to visit your local Health Department office in order to arm yourself with a copy of the health code as it applies to restaurants in your community. While there, try to meet and talk with your own inspector-to-be. Make an appointment, if needed, but *see* him if you possibly can *before* you've begun any vital construction in your kitchen or preparation areas.

Show him your new menu or, at the very least, give the inspector an idea of the cuisine you intend to offer. Present him with a copy of your building plans, showing all rooms on all floors. He may be able to make suggestions to you, in turn, regarding some of your equipment—its size and capacity for the number of people you plan to serve—and its placement within your available space.

Ask him to show you, if he is permitted, the health inspection records of any former restaurant that may have occupied your building. He'll know the site, if it was a food-serving place before, and will tell you, from experience, just what to build in, and what to avoid, in your new construction plans.

All this will be detailed, of course, in your copy of the current health code. You will find, on reading it, that just about all the regulations are sensible, practical, and justified.

To help you comply with the health regulations, here is a checklist of the more important factors for your consideration. Try to *build into* your kitchen, "prep" areas, and dishwashing sections these standards of good sanitation:

- Use quarry tile, brick tile, terrazzo stone, or smooth cement for the flooring. Round off all edges. Allow for a splash area on the walls of about 6 inches. Never install linoleum in these areas.
- Aisle space must be *at least* 30 inches wide.
- Installation of all kitchen equipment must be a recommended number of inches off the floor, apart from the walls, or flush but sealed against them. See your code book for the exact number of inches required in your area. These regulations will make cleaning a lot easier for you.
- Any solder you use should contain no more than 5 percent lead. Show this to your contractor.
- All floor and wall outlets and pipe fittings must be sealed up tightly after hookups. Plug up any holes with steel wool before closing them up.

- Shelving should be of stainless steel, movable, or demountable for easy cleaning. Check your code if you plan to utilize any other material. Never use oilcloth or pressure paper.
- It is recommended that your walls be tiled, smooth cemented, glazed bricked, or wallboard painted with enamel. Never use raw wood. Neither walls nor ceilings should be covered in metal unless all joints are welded tight.
- Hoods and ducts have to be adequate in size to carry off all steam and smoke generated in your cooking area. Seek your architect's or contractor's advice here.
- A grease trap must be installed somewhere on the kitchen water waste line. Ask your plumber.
- All cutting boards are to be removable for scouring.
- A dipper well, with running water, has to be provided for scoops if you plan to serve ice cream.
- Ceiling lights should be adequate, and protected by clear plastic sleeves or other means to prevent any broken glass from contaminating your food.
- There must be good, built-in ventilation, particularly around gas-burning appliances.
- You ought to provide a separate, double-position pot sink, near your cooking area.

Nothing really startling in those rules, is there? Yet, surprisingly, many restaurateurs will try to ignore some of them in order to save a few doubloons. It never works. You'll need to undergo a thorough inspection of your premises by the Health Department in order to secure their permit to operate a restaurant. You cannot open without it. Be prepared, then, by complying with all the regulations as they may apply to you. If in doubt, call up your inspector and ask his advice.

Enclose your garbage area on all four sides, and keep all cans and trash bags tightly lidded or tied up. A garbage bin, as described earlier, is a good move if your receptacles have to be placed near or on the street. Try to secure *daily* trash pickup and removal, even if your operation is relatively small. The less time your garbage stays with you, the better.

As soon as you've gathered together your complete staff —and even before your opening day, during "run-throughs"—set up a cleaning/wiping/mopping routine as an *integral* part of the duties of each member. Your waiters and waitresses are not to consider their shifts to be over, for instance, until they have wiped down all the tables and chairs in their stations, refilled all the sugar, salt, and pepper holders, and set up the entire dining area, in general, ready for use for the next shift. Your dishwasher may be delighted to earn a few more dollars by mopping up or vacuuming the entire restaurant—including, naturally, the kitchen—after you've closed for the night.

Your cooks will be expected to scour and clean all their equipment before leaving, as well as properly put away all food for the night. It will fall on the shoulders of the manager (or you) to see to it that all this is accomplished at the end of *every* shift. These rules are modified, of course, if it is simply a shift change, and you will continue to serve. At closing, however, you must be adamant in your insistence that everything be done *before* your staff is allowed to leave. You'll be astounded how *fast* they can work once they thoroughly understand this!

EXTERMINATORS

Every community of any size has at least two—probably several—professional exterminator firms that will come to your restaurant, inspect all corners of it, inside and outside, and give you an estimate of the cost of pest control. Normally this service will be suggested on a regular visiting basis, usually weekly or semi-monthly, at a time when your place is closed to the public.

Talk personally with these people, so that you will know exactly what they propose to do for you that you may not be able to do for yourself. Be sure their estimates of coverage include any out-of-doors areas, such as your delivery ramp and garbage-disposal enclosures, often initially overlooked. A contract is the norm for this kind of work, but most exterminating firms will be willing to supply you with their services for a few weeks on a trial basis before asking you for a longer commitment.

Since pests of all types are amazingly adaptable, any extermination formulas used should be changed at least two or three times each year. In addition, discuss the variety of pesticides with your professional exterminators to determine that nothing they propose to use in your premises is prohibited by the Health Department for use where food is prepared.

20

REPAIRS
AND
REPLACEMENTS

Imagine the condition of your own home if hundreds and
hundreds of people tramped through it *each day!* Horrify-
ing thought. Especially if one out of three insists on using
the bathroom.

Precisely that scene occurs every day in the hundreds
of thousands of restaurants all over the country. What a
pounding restaurants really do take! It can come as no
surprise, then, that just *occasionally* (hah!) certain
fixtures and equipment will need to be repaired or downright replaced.

What can you do to keep repairs to a minimum? Glad
you asked. Several things. Let's look at a few.

- First of all, choose as many standard, mass-pro-
  duced fixtures as you can without compomising
  your creativity. Don't, for example, purchase a
  special coffee maker handcrafted in Finland, or a
  pattern of wallpaper that is "on sale" because the
  manufacturer is closing it out. Sounds obvious.
  True. But you'd be surprised how easily such obvi-

ous errors can be made when you're rushed, or have a dozen things on your mind *to be attended to right now.*

- Oversupply yourself with certain items you know will break, such as all glassware, salt and pepper shakers, basic silverware, and coffee bowls. The larger quantity you can afford to buy at one time the cheaper, usually, each item becomes. And discount buying is the *proper* way for your restaurant and bar.

- Stock extra wall panels, spindles, floor tiles, wallpaper, blended paints, and special electrical fixtures that will require replacement or matching sooner or later. Otherwise, in later years you'll spend days hunting down replacements for these things.

- Learn as much as you can from your plumber and electrician about your refrigerators, freezers, and compressors and what makes them function. Have them show you where problems usually occur. Simple repairs are frequently all that are required when a piece of this equipment goes out, and they are often *just* that—simple.

- There are leatherette repair kits on the market. If you use any leatherette (or real leather, for that matter) in booths or banquettes, secure a kit and use it while a rift or tear is still comparatively small. Used as directed, these kits will mend beautifully, and your repairs will be hard to detect. Never use colored tape, by the way, except as a stop-gap measure. It won't last a week under normal wear.

- Be sure you understand the exact location of all

turnoffs, cutoff valves, and electrical boxes in your entire system. Study the directions for handling them, and post a chart on a nearby wall detailing instructions for others to follow in case you're not on hand in an emergency. Instruct everybody where to turn off the water main if ever needed. This is important, since such mains are often purposefully located in out-of-traffic places so they won't be disturbed accidentally.

- Take the time to instruct all new cooks and dishwashers exactly how their equipment is to be maintained and cleaned. Insist they do it themselves. Be patient. Instruct them again if they do it wrong, until maintenance procedures become a part of their regular, daily routines. You'll save thousands each year this way.

- Check your robbery or burglary insurance policy for vandalism protection coverage. Chances are you have it. While it won't save time, it will save you a good deal of money for replacements.

- Ask your waiters, waitresses, and bartenders to supply their own uniforms. (*You* must supply your cooks, busboys, and dishwashers with fresh uniforms every shift.) Unless you have a specifically designed uniform in mind, this will save you thousands per year in laundry rentals alone.

- Avoid wicker or cane-bottomed chairs and stools. They're handsome, but they cannot stand up to constant use.

- Make all repairs as quickly as possible so they don't get worse. This is probably the best advice of all. Procrastination only makes a heavy repair bill larger still.

21

INVENTORY AND GUEST CHECK CONTROL

Inventory control is one of those awesome-sounding job titles that can fill your mind with horrendous thoughts of endless reams of paperwork. Or beef filets finding their way out the back door. Cloak and dagger stuff. But it needn't be made difficult, really. Let's take an easy overview.

What, then, does "inventory" mean? It simply refers to a list you make of all the foodstuffs and liquor you have on hand at a given time. Those items will be resting in your storerooms, in refrigerators, and in your freezers (or, in the case of your bar, on display). You make a list, for example, of cases or half-cases of tomatoes, bottles of wine, number of pounds of a cut of beef, number of fish fillets—that sort of thing. You do it when least busy, or closed to the public, so your list has a stable starting point.

Once you have these lists made up, you can begin the "control" part of your inventory. All *it* means, however, is that you will do one or all of the following with those lists, depending on your aims and reasons for making the lists in the first place:

- Check your inventory against the daily bills that have come in with the individual orders from your purveyors.
- Make sure that someone you trust—or you yourself—weighs all incoming foodstuffs, especially meats, and count all cases *on delivery*. This is simply common sense.
- Check your list against yesterday's guest checks, noting what was ordered on each. Subtract the amounts of the various foods sold from your inventory list. The resulting figure, within reasonable limits, should be what you *now* have on hand, if you haven't received any further deliveries. If you have, compensate.
- Check your bar receipts against the remaining inventory on hand. Count all half-bottles as well both times.

And that is the essence of the awesome "Inventory Control." Not nearly as worrisome as it sounded, hmm? It *does* take time, however, to do this personally. Allow for that, and don't be rushed.

Some of the newer cash registers will perform a good deal of this work for you, providing you with a constant updating of your basic inventory. But remember: Any data that comes *out* of such a register must be punched *in* somewhere along the line, and that takes a few seconds each time the register is rung up.

What about controlling guest checks, you say? The best guest check controls involve numbered, preprinted cards, and/or an honest food checker. But food checkers are expensive to hire. Such positions are found primarily in huge, impersonal restaurants or hotel dining rooms. Most smaller establishments cannot afford such a person, and have no space to spare, anyway. So they rely on a system of numbered guest checks, with carbon copies to do the work. Systems vary, but this is basically how they all work.

Guest checks numbered *in exact order* are assigned to each waiter and waitress and to the bartender. Note is made in a book of the blank check numbers issued to each person. The owner or manager keeps that book. Each guest check must be used, canceled, or returned unused —and back in numerical order—at the end of each server's duty period. *All* cards issued must be accounted for. These, then, can be compared with the used "dupes" that the cooks keep after they have filled each order.

Using a cash register that has several lettered buttons, each representing a different server (A, B, C, D at least), a numbered card is inserted and rung up on a lettered key for all liquor, beer, or wine that is ordered. When the bill is paid, the same *total* amount is rung up *again,* using a different key. In this way, you have two totals, one for liquor sold and another for liquor paid for. They should be exactly the same.

There is, of course, no substitute for vigilance on your part. Honesty *does* prevail most of the time, but handling money is a constant source of temptation to anyone who finds himself "a bit short" on occasion. It is difficult— under *any* system—to catch up with either food or liquor *given* away, with no guest check ever involved in the transaction. (This is why you must compare your duplicate checks from your chef's spindle.) Your inventory lists are the best guide in that situation, both practically *and* psychologically. Don't hesitate to immediately discharge employees caught cheating. They will cry, and promise you anything—but they will, most likely, do it again.

The more sophisticated your cash register system, the more difficult it will be to cheat you; and your controls will be proportionately easier to maintain, once established. How much you can afford for a cash register will depend, as usual, on your budget. But if at all possible, buy a machine that has at least *some* controls built into it. Most restaurants do not need a top-of-the-line register, but without some controls you will be cheated sooner or later in your career. Check out used machines as well as the newest ones. Many times you'll be able to pick up a register that has seen only a year or two of service at half the cost of a comparable new one. But remember: A really good register will pay for itself in short order.

You now know the rudiments of inventory control and guest check control. With this briefing, you should be able to understand the details of most systems.

Wasn't all that complex, was it?

22

HIRING
YOUR
STAFF

You have reached the stage now when you're going to need to hire help. You will find it easier and more expedient to advertise and interview prospective cooks and a manager, if you will require one, about a month or so before your projected actual opening date. This will give both you *and* them a chance to meet each other and consult in an atmosphere of relaxation rather than urgency.

On your part, you can conduct two or three sessions, if needed, in order to find the kind of staff—both in ability and personality—that you feel will fit best. On their part, the staff you choose will have sufficient time to give their current employers a decent notice period, keeping *everybody* happy.

If you or your partners are not planning to be on the premises of your new restaurant all the time, the most important member of your staff will be the manager. Be sure to select and hire this employee early enough to be with you in the final weeks before opening. Not only will it help him or her to become familiar with all your problems and aspirations, but you two will have the chance to work together creatively. You will get to know each other and—not least of all—you'll have the opportunity to determine if he or she is, indeed, the kind of person you can trust to act in your stead. You will hire no one *more* important to your success than your manager, not even your cooks. If the manager's duties include inventory, cash handling, and some book work, this is doubly true. Give yourself ample time, therefore, to find just the right person for this position.

Next in importance—and not to be downgraded in the least—are your chefs or cooks. Depending on your individual menu, your capacity, and your hours, you will need a *minimum* of one or two cooks and, probably, an assistant cook for each. If you're planning to serve even a modified haute cuisine, you'll need one or two *fully qualified* chefs, with cooks in training as assistants. And you must be prepared to pay them wages well above the average.

In any case, the cooks you select should be delighted to do some test cooking for you, either in the restaurant's kitchen or in your own home. Familiarize each of them with your menu requirements, then give each a free hand within those limits. You'll be astounded—maybe delighted—with the results, and your cooks, if they've done their preparations properly, will be proud. Of course, the bad apples will show up this way, too. You can't lose.

Naturally, if you're opening a short-order kitchen, or a pancake house, you will be able to accomplish your test cooking on the spot, since it will most likely follow a formula. Here you'll want to know if your cooks can understand a recipe rather than demonstrate creativity.

When you advertise, try to be as explicit as possible. Spend a dollar or two more for an extra advertising line, saving yourself a hundred misguided phone calls. State the hours, days per week, and salary if desirable to do so. List the skills required (or not required, if you can train), and the benefits you offer other than wages. Mention in your ad just *when* to call or come by the restaurant, and ask for a résumé for all but the simplest jobs.

Actual interviewing is not easy. It is a time-consuming process, and psychologically wearing on all concerned, not least of all on you, the employer. You are dealing with human beings, whose emotions are all up front. Each is undergoing the difficult task of selling him- or herself to a total stranger. You *must* be patient, therefore, even when you least feel like it; and decently kind, even when you know the prospective employee will not fit in the minute he or she starts talking.

Interviewing usually comes down to a "weeding out" process. You talk to each new applicant in turn, making notes as you go along. You then reread your notes and résumés, and call back your choices at a later date for a follow-up—and more detailed—interview. This system seems to work best.

Never, never advertise for more than one position at a given time unless there are two of you to conduct the interviews. You need full concentration on a particular job when talking to—for example—bartenders, without having to shift to waitresses or busboys, and *their* qualifications, all in the same afternoon. Simply stagger your appointment days.

In most cities, there are restaurant employment agencies. Federal and state employment offices in your area

A crowd of applicants.

can also supply qualified help. Both are especially good at supplying young people, eager and ready for training, for your lesser skilled jobs. Call them.

Experience usually costs more. Youth is usually the most adaptable. The time you have at your disposal to teach, to train, will determine how much reliance you can put into unskilled—but willing—restaurant help. However, except in the areas of management and, perhaps, cooking (other than short-order meals), very little training is really *necessary* to most restaurant operations. In all cases, you must take time with each new employee until he or she is able to adapt to your regimen and scheduling.

Young people are fast learners, and possess all the extra energy needed to keep you humming all day long if your cooking needs are relatively simple. Fast-food establishments sometimes seem to be staffed entirely with teenagers, most of whom do a splendid job. Positions as assistant cooks, kitchen help (preparation), dishwashers, waiters, and waitresses are the easy-to-learn jobs in most restaurants. They will be the easiest on your personnel budget, too.

Have your entire staff hired at least three or four days prior to your formal opening date. Each day prepare some of the dishes that will be featured on your menu. Start everyone working at his or her job *before* the public is invited. In this way, you can iron out the kinks, find out who really works best together, and familiarize each person with his or her duties. Your staff will, in particular, learn where to find things, such as the peppermill, ice water, extra bar rags, replacement electric bulbs, and extra cups and saucers. Your cooks will be able to secure those extra pans and spoons no one thought they'd need. It's your very own "shakedown cruise."

Then, when you do open your doors to your (eagerly awaiting) public, each of your staff will know how to charm them.

23

ADVERTISING
AND
PUBLICITY

There is no better advertising or publicity in this world than word of mouth. Unfortunately, that can work both ways.

To ensure that your new restaurant gets the best press, then, give your neighborhood something *positive* to talk about right from the beginning. Even while you're building the place, while carpenters are measuring and hammering, clear a space in your otherwise soaped-up windows and announce to one and all just what it is that you are creating here. Do this on a colorful poster, with an eye-catching headline if you can. Be inventive and friendly in your announcements. Vary them from week to week, building up excitement for your anticipated opening date.

Hook up your coffee urns as soon as possible. Then invite passersby in for a free cup of coffee and a look-see at your evolving work. Only do this, of course, when you are on the premises yourself. It's a marvelous way to get to know your future customers personally, and it gives *them* a small sense of participation in your new restaurant, too.

As the opening day approaches, call all the local newspapers and invite them to come by with cameras. Dress your chefs in gleaming whites with tall chefs' hats worn at a jaunty angle, and suggest that they be photographed, smiling, while standing at the new stove. Have some refreshments handy. And place a few ads in all the papers that gave you some publicity. Take a series of short radio advertisements, announcing your opening dates and the kind of delectables you'll be serving. Ask your neighbors to come by for a complimentary glass, or cup, of cheer by way of saying hello to each other. Run off copies of your menu on simple, thin, colored paper—then hire an attractive person to hand them out to passersby on the sidewalk.

Just prior to opening, you might consider the advisability of holding two or three private cocktail parties (with food) on your new premises for certain groups you'd like to see more often. It's a very nice way to say thank you, as well, to a good number of people who have been particularly helpful to you in any way. You'll never have a better excuse for getting them all together. Besides, everyone loves a party.

On opening day itself, you will be packed to the doorways. To help everyone keep calm and not become impatient, you might provide some simple, giveaway souvenirs of the occasion. This can act both as a promotion and as a solace for all the inevitable confusion of opening day. A free coffee mug—with your name and logo on it—will pay handsome dividends for months to come. A paper chef's hat, or party favors, or balloons for the youngsters will please both them *and* their parents. Flowers, usually for the ladies, are a sure hit. Be inventive, but—whatever you choose to do—be certain your souvenirs will also serve as a reminder that your new restaurant is now open for business.

During your first few months of operation, try to include as many "tie-ins" with local events as you can. If it's Strawberry Week in your community, not only feature strawberry desserts, but create a special low price for them, that week only. Allow a small discount to local high school or college students on certain days, or during less-trafficked hours. Feature Irish stew and corned beef and cabbage on Saint Patrick's Day. (Offer free seltzer the morning after!)

Advertising and publicity can and should be genuine fun for all, yourself included. If you can think up a promotion that both you and your staff will enjoy doing, the chances are that your patrons will be delighted with it, too.

Beat the drums. Toot your own horn. Let 'em know you're there. After all, you *are* in show business, aren't you?

24

RELATIONSHIPS— YOU WITH YOUR STAFF, YOUR STAFF WITH YOUR PATRONS

Since it will be physically impossible for you to be on hand at your restaurant *all* the time, it is of paramount importance for you to establish, at the outset, a firm chain of command. Your top officer, next to you, is always your manager, who will represent you whenever you are absent. This is a position of authority. You must *defer* to your manager on certain matters now and again, in order to reinforce his or her position with the rest of the staff. *Always* support your manager in front of your staff. If you do disagree, work out any problems you may have together (in privacy, preferably in your office) and then allow your manager to announce any changes on which you have decided. In this way your staff will come to appreciate your chain of command, and to accept your manager's judgments as though they were your own. Supervising your restaurant in your absence requires a *firm,* but understanding, hand at the helm to keep your staff happy, cooperative, and efficient.

A touchy situation can occur in your kitchens. Your chef, and the cooks, are usually considered the masters of *their* own domains. However, there must be harmony, trust, and empathy between your manager and your cooks in order to achieve a smooth operation. You can best bring this about by spelling out to your manager and your cooks *exactly* what you expect the responsibilities of each to be, so that neither will try to invade the other's domain. Set down rules, for example, for ordering food and supplies, and for checking them out when the orders are delivered. In the kitchen, your chef is the chief. The *chef* is responsible for his or her own output and that of any of the assistant cooks, and should be allowed to handle this task with authority. Naturally, your chef must defer to you or your manager should a real conflict arise, but your aim must always be to so define their individual areas of influence that they will be able to work together easily.

Peace at any price is *not* a good rule, however, in a restaurant. If an employee and your manager really cannot get along, one or the other must go. Do not put up with bickering under any circumstances. Your entire staff will be disrupted in short order, and even your patrons will notice it before long.

In due course, designate one of your waiters or waitresses as a head waiter, and begin to groom him or her as an assistant manager as well. You will then have someone in your organization who will be able to take over management duties in the event of illness, vacations, or any emergencies. An increase in salary—together with an understanding that the position of manager, should it become vacant, would go to this person—should accompany this selection, in order to establish still another level in your command chain.

Treat everyone with dignity. Thank each member of your staff, personally, when they have worked especially hard for you during a rush period or an emergency. And, if you possibly can, add an on-the-spot bonus to your congratulations as well. It needn't be much, but it is tangible proof that their efforts were appreciated. A little profit sharing goes a long way.

Cleanliness means more than filed fingernails and a fresh uniform. It is an attitude of mind, actually, that could be best summed up as *pride* in one's work. If the members of your staff are relatively happy in what they're doing, you will rarely find it necessary to speak to them about their appearance. Her hair will be combed, his shoes shined (assuming he's not working in the kitchen), and neither will be chewing gum.

Friendliness is an art and can be learned. Your waiters and waitresses, your manager, and your bartender should all try to learn your customers' names. Nothing is more flattering, more status conferring, to your patrons. As time goes by, a good server or bartender will learn particular preferences of individual customers. Thus a bartender will be able to ask a 'regular', when he comes in, if he'd like his "usual"—and give it to him. Or a cup of coffee can be served and waiting for a steady customer even before she sits down, with the sugar and cream alongside as she likes it. Such little attentions—so easy to do—and accompanied with a genuine smile, will keep your restaurant a crowded, friendly stopping-off place all day long. Tips will be great. Your revenue will be up, too.

If you must be an absentee owner—and sometimes it simply cannot be avoided—it is doubly important for you to hire a manager you can trust, and to *pay* this person *well.* You will be asking him or her, in effect, to take on all *your* responsibilities. By making that additional effort well worthwhile, you just may be able to run your empire from afar.

Even if you've created three or four restaurants, or more, and therefore cannot be at each one very often, try to keep in *constant* touch with your managers. Let them and your staff know you care, and care a lot, and are not just concentrating on the other restaurants to their exclusion.

Vacations are a must for both your staff *and* you. After your restaurant has been open about six months or so, and everything's running swimmingly (or even if it's *not*), you'd better plan to get away for a week or two. *Far* away, where no one can reach you to ask you even a single question. You'll be amazed, probably, how well it will all run while you're gone. You'll find answers to some of your problems from the vantage point of being removed from everyday involvements. And, best of all, you'll renew your sense of creativity by being able to look at your operation at a distance, to see it, now, as others see it.

Staff vacations ought to be a package of your operating policy. At least two weeks per year, with pay, should be allowed everyone who's on your permanent schedule. If you have some major repairs to accomplish—a new flooring, for example, or rearrangement of your kitchen—you might consider closing entirely for two weeks, allowing everyone to take their vacations at the same time. Otherwise, it's best to stagger staff vacations, usually in the summertime, on a schedule that you make out *with* each person, individually, earlier in the year. This way you never have to close down, and spoil the dining habits of your blessed regulars.

A birthday—to the one who's having it—is an important date. For each of us, a birth date proclaims a certain uniqueness. The day is always special. For the restaurant that prides itself on being run as a "family," birthdays can be the occasion for a small celebration right in the restaurant, during the slower part of the day. A cake can be baked—and topped with candles, of course. A bottle or two of champagne can be popped, with everyone in sight (including patrons) sharing a wee taste. "Happy Birthday" will, inevitably, be sung, off key but lustily. And the person whose birthday it is that day will be delightfully embarrassed, of course, but inwardly, where it counts most, awfully glad he or she chose *you* to work for.

25

HOW
TO HANDLE
YOUR SUCCESS

Well, you did it. You really *did* it. There stands the gleaming, smart new restaurant of your dreams. It's built now, and it's beautiful, a monument to your creativity and determination.

Of *course* it will be a success. And why shouldn't it be? The very determination that took you this far will see you in triumph for the rest of the way as well.

Now it's time for you to begin to enjoy your new role as owner and proprietor. The problems of planning, approvals, and construction are over. They won't concern you again unless you decide to expand. Pleasant thought, that.

Ah, but *is* it? It's usually best to give your new restaurant a year, at least, of everyday operation just as it is, before you begin any serious consideration of plans for expansion. You'll find you have peaks *and* valleys in any given week's output. They're pounding on your doors even before you open on weekends, you say? You're jammed to the rafters on Friday, Saturday, and Sunday nights? Splendid. You're obviously doing *something* right, and you're apparently popular in your community. So you certainly ought to arrange to build on, expand, make the place larger in order to accommodate just that many more at a time, don't you think?

Not necessarily. Consider *all* the implications of expansion first. Increased dining room space will mean, naturally, increased kitchen capacity, too. You'll have to add another stove in all probability, more refrigerators, another broiler or two, and still another deep-fryer. Hoods will have to be stretched, exhaust fans enlarged, and your fire prevention system replaced with a larger size. Are you ready for all that again?

Then, too, your patrons may be knocking your doors down on weekends, but where—oh, *where*?—are they on Mondays, Tuesdays, and Wednesdays? You and your expanded restaurant will probably be open for business on those days, too—will you be able to utilize your increased space then? If not, could you close off some portion of the dining room without having to light or heat it? Air-condition it?

A larger kitchen also implies a larger staff in it. Good cooks, as you know, are not easy to come by, nor very easy on the budget when you do find them. Does your expansion justify the increased payroll costs, do you think?

Does your neighborhood tend to be somewhat cliquish? Do they tend to rush off and mob *any* new spot that opens? If so, can you be sure you'll need all that increased footage when some new competition—it's bound to happen if *you're* so obviously successful—opens its doors just down the avenue?

Answer all these questions to yourself just as honestly as you can before you even consider enlarging your current capacity. If you're still bullish after all that soul-searching, then, by all means, plunge ahead. You've undoubtedly created the most welcomed restaurant in the entire neighborhood. Congratulations, again!

Another possibility open to you at this stage, of course, is opening another restaurant in another part of town. Drawing on the knowledge gained with this endeavor, and your ability, now, to assess the costs of the job, your next restaurant should easily be capable of repeating the success of your first. Thus are restaurant chains born.

Until then, however, concentrate your energies where you are. Involve yourself in local community affairs. Offer your place, or a corner of it, for neighborhood meetings or discussions during nonrush hours. Be sure to be there yourself. As a proprietor, and a very visible one at that, many local people will form the habit of looking to you for decisions of all kinds. You are, being a restaurateur, the most approachable of all bosses. You will automatically become a force in your community, whether you thought of yourself in that way or not.

You may as well enjoy it. Together with your business neighbors, plan a block party once or twice each year. Celebrate spring, as a suggestion. Decorate the street with flowers. Set up some of your tables and chairs outside to accommodate the crowds. Create special dishes for the occasion. Plan a Halloween Fete, with pumpkins, and, perhaps, a small live band to keep the youngsters agreeably occupied that peculiar evening. It will all reflect handsomely on you and your restaurant, making your place even more popular. And don't be surprised if you find yourself immensely enjoying the efforts you will make in bringing it all about. Community actions of this caliber can be great fun.

Hand in hand in importance with community acceptance is the consideration of your own staff. The loyalty of your team can only be earned over the years. Keeping their needs in mind as well as your own, however, will go a long way toward making you a dependable employer. If you've had an especially good year, realize that you did not accomplish this all alone by any means. Be generous in giving your deserving staff members Christmas or vacation bonuses, by way of saying thank you for a job well done. Review all wages once each year—more often if inflation continues—giving increases, as best you are able, to all your loyal staff. Develop a friendly ear when they come to you with personal problems. Help them if you possibly can with advances of salary (but *never* loans) or leaves of absence. You may be Mom in the Kitchen to your patrons, but you're Big Daddy to your staff. It could only happen in the restaurant business! Encourage it. This is your surest route to lasting loyalty.

Now that you and your restaurant are a crashing success, and the place has begun to lose that brand-new look, what's your next move? You have several options, all of them delightful.

One, of course, is to stay right where you are, run the place with pleasure, and try to keep abreast of all the changes in this business. Be flexible over the years. Keep your restaurant as vital and interesting a place as it was in the very beginning. Never let down on any of your standards for a moment. If you can do this, you will continue to make a handsome living for as long as you like.

You may, indeed, find it profitable to expand, or start

up a sister restaurant in another part of town. Try to finance each new unit on its *own*, however, if you do build more than one. You do not want to run the risk of endangering your first restaurant should anything go awry with the second. Never sacrifice one to the other. Take your time. Be sure each operation is on its own secure financial base *before* starting off on another. In this way, you'll avoid the recurrent dangers of overexpansion.

Finally, you can sell your going restaurant—at a hefty profit, of *course*!—to someone who hasn't the patience, time, or know-how to build one up, as you did, from a barnlike beginning. Your profit, moreover, will only be taxed as a long-term gain, allowing you some good capital for reinvestments. If you enjoy the creative aspects of planning a new restaurant, following it through to opening day, and seeing it set up with smooth-running management, then this is a highly lucrative way to invest your time and money. Almost everybody dreams of owning his or her own restaurant sometime. There will never be any lack of buyers, therefore, for a visibly successful operation.

Right now, though, why not lean back, pour out a glass of the bubbly, and toast your handsome new restaurant. You've been through a lot, some of it fun, some of it a bit of a headache, but it's all accomplished now. Your dream is a beautiful reality.

Cheers. Try not to look too smug for the photographers.

APPENDIX

A QUICK REFERENCE GUIDE TO EQUIPMENT, SUPPLIES, AND COSTS

The listings that follow are close duplicates of those made and examined more thoroughly throughout the book. They are pulled together for you here as a guide, and perhaps a reminder, of the supplies and equipment you will need to consider for your own restaurant.

Pencil onto these lists any special equipment you will require for your own particular establishment. Cross out any you won't need. You will then have a complete working list of your own from which to figure your costs and accomplish your ordering.

With regard to the column headed "Approximate Costs," bear in mind that these prices are only meant as a *guide*, and are by no means final. Your own costs may prove to be considerably lower, since each figure given here is based on the best available, *top*-quality equipment and supplies, and by its very nature can only serve as a general estimate. When possible, excellent used and reconditioned equipment can often be found at a 40 to 50 percent reduction. It would be well worth your while to check this out first.

Now, when all your individual needs are listed and finally priced, I have to tell you to add 10 percent to cover the costs of taxes, transportation, shipping charges, and various miscellaneous expenses neither you nor I can think of right now, but which *will* occur.

Good hunting.

Major Kitchen Equipment	Approximate Cost (New, Top-Quality)
Heavy-duty stove (with six burners and a baking oven)	$975
Overhead broiler (separate from stove)	$725
Grill, (separate from Stove) (24″)	$350
Deep-fryer (electric or gas, large, floor model)	$950
Hood, exhaust fan, and vents over the entire cooking area	$150 p/foot
Extra set of hood filters	$10 each
Fan duct to the outside	$150 p/foot
3-compartment preparation sink and drainboard	$325
Hooded 4-foot sandwich board (4′) atop a lowboy refrigerator	$1,400
Freezers: Walk-in (6′ × 6′)	$3,900
Walk-in (10′ × 10′)	$5,000
Standard 2-door upright	$2,300
Reach-down (4′)	$1,200
Heavy-duty toaster	$375
Stainless-steel shelving	$60 p/foot
Steam table (4′)	$300
Refrigerators: Walk-in (6′ × 6′)	$3,400
Walk-in (10′ × 10′)	$4,800
Standard 2-door upright	$1,800
Reach-in lowboy (4′)	$1,300
Large-size pots, griddles, pans, and open containers	Prices will vary according to menu and size of the restaurant

Pass-through/over counter	See your contractor
Double heat lamps for above	$95
Stainless-steel preparation table (6')	$250
Fire protection system, cooking area	$300 p/foot
Knife holder	$25
Slicing machine (large)	$1,600
Fire extinguishers	$35 each
Garbage bag holder racks	$25 each
Bun warmer (optional)	$525
Electric mixer (20 qt.) (optional)	$24,00
Microwave oven: Small (600 watts)	$550
Large(1,500 watts)	$1,500

Dining Room Equipment

Tables: Formica 24″ × 24″	$25 each
30″ × 30″	$38 each
Chairs	$25 to $75
Leatherette booths (double)	$170 +
Banquettes (leatherette)	$45 p/ft.
Lamps: Table	—
Overhead	—
Door signs (lighted "EXIT")	$20
Music: Stereo with remote speakers	$500 +
Jukebox	They pay *you*
Cash register	$1,000 to $5,000
Guest checks (fitted to register)	25 p/carton
Floor coverings: Inlaid wood	See your carpenter
Industrial carpeting	$15 p/ft. +
Industrial floor tile	$5 p/ft.
Quarry tile	$12 p/ft.

Salad bar (refrigerated lowboy) (4')	$1,400
Table coverings: Cloth	Supplied by laundry serv.
Paper placemats	$12 p/carton
Wood or laminate	Varies by thickness
Waiters' stand, incorporating:	
Coffee maker/warmer (5 place)	$500
Water fountain/pitchers	—
Glassware shelving (glass)	$4 p/ft.
Silverware trays	$25
Napkin bin	$10
Peppermills	$25 (large)
Mounted copy of the menu	—
Bun warmer (optional)	$525
Glass-fronted refrigerator (may be located in kitchen, however)	$1,300.
Silverware (Begin with *at least* 2 1/2 times your seating capacity)	
Spoons: Tea or soup	$3 + doz.
Knives: Regular or steak	$5 doz.
Butter	$4 doz.
Forks: Regular or salad	$5 + doz.
Lobster/crab	$4 doz.
Glassware: Water (10 oz.)	$8 doz.
Juice (5 oz.)	$7 doz.
Dishware (*Minimum* needs, 2 1/2 times your seating capacity; buy from *open stock*)	
Serving platters	$12 to $25 doz.
Salad platters/bowls	$12 to $18 doz.
Soup bowls (large) (need less)	$30 doz.
Bread and butter plates	$15 doz.
Dessert plates	$15 doz.
Fruit cups (need less)	$18 doz.

Cups (need more—early chipping)	$15 to 22 doz.
Saucers	$12 doz.
Monkey Dishes (need less)	$15 doz.
Creamers (standard) (need less)	$30 doz.
Sugar holders	$12 doz.
Salt and pepper shakers (regular)	$3 doz.
Ashtrays (glass)	$3 doz.
Napkin holders (fast food)	Supplied by paper distributor free
Customer condiment trays (fast food)	$38 doz.
Trash bag holders/racks	$25 each
Bus trays	$4 each
Bus tray stand (stainless steel)	$125
First aid/choking poster	$2 each

Ice Cream Fountain

Counter (with 3-position sink)	Varies by contractor
Stools: With backs	$30 to $60 each
Without backs	$20 to $45 each
Reach-in Fountain (6 to 8 holes plus holding trays, dispensers, and drain)	$3,500 +
Extra soda dispensers	See soft drink distributor
Coffee stand/brewer (5 place)	$500
Coffee Urns, Twin (3 gal.)	$1,700
Milkshake machine Single	$140
Three-header	$360
Ice machine (200 pounds)	$1,400 (or rent)
Hot chocolate/iced tea jet spray	$350 to $650
Milk dispenser/refrigerator	See your milkman (may be free)

Glass-fronted refrigerator	$1,300
Lowboy (3', single door)	$900
Pizza oven	$1,800

Bar Equipment

Your bar itself, the top back bar, including mirrors, and your lower back bar skeleton will have to be custom made for you, either individually or by your carpenter. Costs should be related to size alone. In addition, you'll need:

2 reach-in lowboy refrigerators	$900 to $1,300 each
Cash register	$1,000 to $5,000
Guest checks (fitted to register)	$25 p/carton
3-position sink and heating unit	$300
2 drainboards (stainless steel) for above	$75 each
Speed racks (1 or 2)	$40 each
Wine racks (optional)	$20 p/foot
Draft beer dispenser and drain (double)	$1,800 (see your distributor)
Ice bin (open-topped, stainless-steel)	$120
Seltzer dispenser (snake)	$250 (or rent)
Glassware shelving (service stand)	$4 p/ft.
Ice machine (200 pounds)	$1,400 (or rent)
Trash/used bottle holders (racks)	$25 each
Skid-proof floor slats	See your carpenter
Telephone (optional)	—
Glassware	
Highball (10 to 12 oz.) (12 doz.)	$8 doz.
Beer mugs (12 to 14 oz.) (9 doz.)	$14 doz.

Wine (10 to 12 oz.) (6 doz.)	$12 doz.
Old-fashioned, 8–10 oz. (8 doz.)	$12 doz.
Brandy (8 to 12 oz.) (3 doz.)	$15 doz.
Pony (2 oz.) (3 doz.)	$12 doz.
Whiskey Sour (4 1/2 to 6 oz.) (6 doz.)	$12 doz.
Shot 1 1/2 to 2 oz. (1 doz.)	$5 doz.
Martini 4 oz. (6 doz.)	$12 doz.
Champagne, 6–8 oz. (2 doz.)	$16 doz.

Optional glassware:

Sherry (4 to 6 oz.)	$12 doz.
Pilsner (12 oz.)	$14 doz.
Cocktail (6 oz.)	$10 doz.
Punch Cup (6 to 8 oz.)	$18 doz.

To be ready to serve, your bar must also have the following: 2 paring knives, boxes of stirrers, 2 to 4 corkscrews, martini pitcher, jigger measure, ice tongs, blender, long-handled bar spoons (several), funnel, glass shakers (16 oz.), strainer, and mixing glass (at least 2), coasters, bar rags, juicer, cocktail napkins, ice scoop, and a cutting board.

You'll need, in addition, a good supply of: jars of small onions, olives, and cherries, tabasco sauce, oranges, limes, and lemons, nutmeg, grenadine syrup, salt, superfine sugar, Rose's lime juice, tinned tomato juice, Worcestershire sauce, cinnamon sticks, eggs, heavy cream, soap powder, and disinfectant

Draft beer can be ordered by the

keg or the half-keg. The latter is the most useful.

Buy a liquor control inventory book with loose-leaf pages.

Approx. $25

LIQUOR, BEER, WINE— MINIMUM REQUIREMENTS FOR START-UP

Stock 1 dozen cases of each of the top three most popular beers in your area, plus 4 cases each of a dark beer, and the leading imported brand, in addition to your draft beer. If you do not plan to feature draft beer, then treble this order.

Costs for beer, liquor and wine vary in each state according to its taxes

Purchase at *least* 3 cases of the following wines. Taste-test your brands first. You can add to these later.

Dry white wine (California)
Robust red wine (California)
Sparkling wine (optional)
Italian red wine
French/German white wine
French Burgundy/Beaujolais wine
Sherry (1/2 case)
Champagne (1/2 case)

Liquor: Your local distributors will have a selection of "house" brands for most of the often-called-for liquors. Taste-test these, and buy several cases each of scotch, gin, vodka, rum, bourbon, and American blended whiskey. Use these whenever a particular brand is not requested.

In addition to the "house" brands, you should plan to open with the following:

Vodka: American (1 case)
          Imported (1/2 case)

Scotch: 4 to 5 top brands, both light and heavy (1 case each)

American blended whiskey: 2 to 3 top brands (1 case each)

Canadian whiskey (1/2 case)

Bourbon: 1 or 2 blends, plus one Tennessee or sour mash (1 case each)

Irish whiskey (2 to 3 bottles)

Tequila (1/2 case)

Campari (1 bottle)

Gin: 2 American, 2 imported brands (1 case each)

Rum: 1 light, 1 gold, 1 dark (1/2 case each)

Brandies: V.S.O.P. Cognac (3 to 4 bottles)
          California (1/2 case)
          Calvados (1 bottle)
          Kirsch (1 bottle)
          Cherry/apricot (1 bottle, each; optional)

Amaretto (2 bottles)

Coffee liqueur (1 bottle; optional)

B & B (2 bottles)

Grand Marnier (2 bottles)

Cream liqueur (1/2 case)
Irish Mist (1 bottle; optional)
Drambuie (2 bottles)
Sambuca Romana (1 bottle; optional)
Crème de cacao (white) (1 bottle)
Crème de menthe (white) (1 bottle)
Dry vermouth (3 cases)
Sweet vermouth (1 case)

Major Equipment— Dishwashing Area

Electric dishwashing machine (400 to 500 pieces p/hr., with built-in booster)	$2,300
Rinse arm	$175
2 drain boards (31') (stainless-steel)	$75 each
Grease trap	$350
2 or more garbage container holders	$25 each
Stacking table (stainless-steel)	$275
Drainage shelves (stainless-steel) (optional)	$75 each
Storage shelves (stainless-steel)	$75 each
Hot water heater	See your plumber
Booster (optional)	$600
Bus trays	$5 each
Bus tray carts (on wheels)	$19–125
Wall fan	See your electrician
6 plastic silverware holders	$5 each
3-position sink (stainless-steel)	$300
Nonskid rubber floor mat (5')	$70

Storage Equipment

You'll need built-in open shelving for:
  Tinned & boxed foods

Dishware, glassware, and extra
  silver
Liquor
Clean laundry
You'll need off-the-floor bins for:
  Paper goods (in boxes)
  Soaps
  Potatoes
  Soiled laundry
  Cases of beer and wine
  Extra tanks of seltzer or setups

Storage freezers: Walk-in (6' × 6')		$3,900
Walk-in (10' × 10')		$5,000
Standard 2-door upright		$2,300
Storage refrigerators:		
Walk-in (6' × 6')		$3,400
Walk-in (10' × 10')		$4,800
Standard 2-door upright		1,800

Outside Garbage Disposal

Set aside an area on your grounds
at least 6 × 6 feet, if possible, for
garbage. (Make certain a truck can
reach it.) Ask your carpenter to estimate costs for following:
Garbage bin
Fencing (with gate)
Cement flooring

Office Equipment

Desk (full size)	$300 to $600
Desk lamp	$50
2 legal-width 2-drawer filing cabinets	$85 each

2 chairs	$25 to $75 each
Telephone	—
Overhead book shelves	$4 p/ft.
Calculator (with tape)	$100 to $300

Restrooms and Dressing Room

If not already provided, this is an area for discussion with your plumber and carpenter/contractor. These rooms need not be much more than utilitarian unless you want them to be. Be sure your electrician installs a proper wall fan in each room. This is usually a buildings code requirement, but often overlooked.

Insurance

Required by law: Workman's compensation

Costs vary according to community regulations and experience

Must have: Health/hospital
Liability (people and product)
Fire
Desirable: Vandalism and holdup
Business interruption

Licenses

Permit to run a restaurant

Costs minimal once all the various requirements are met

Health Department certificate
Fire Department inspection permit
Buildings Department approvals
Highway/Roadway Commission permit
Consumer's Affairs certificate
Place of assembly permit (some states)
Historic Society (if required)
Alcoholic beverage license

Most States ask $1,000 to $2,000 p/yr. Seasonal licenses are often halved

Miscellaneous

Weighing scale (for all deliveries) — $50
Extra glass coffee serving bowls. — $8 each
Leatherette repair kit — $20
Extra calculator and cash register tapes — $2 each
Extra guest checks — $25 p/carton
Replacement rubber rinse arm for dishwashing machine — $175

INDEX

dining room *(continued)*
major equipment for, 87–104,
191–193. *See also specific
item*
discounts, 177
dishes, 90
dishwashing area, 121
major equipment for, 65–73,
198. *See also specific item*
dishwashing machine, 66–68, 79,
111
dispensers
draft beer, 36–37
miscellaneous, 97
seltzer, 39–40
soda, 96–97
doors, double swinging, 61,
103
drain table, 70
drainage, 79, 80–81
drainboards, 36, 68–69
dressing rooms, 75–76, 86,
200
drinks. *See also* liquor
complimentary, in
advertising, 176
ducting, 51

electric mixer, 63–64
electrician, 79, 81, 128
employees. *See* staff
engineer, 107, 121–122
equipment, major, 47–105. *See
also specific area; item*
cost of, 190–192, 193–194,
198–200, 201
repair and replacement of,
2–3, 163–166
exhaust fan, 53–54, 112
expansion, restaurant, 183–186

exterior
designing, 108
and regulations, 12, 23
exterminators, 162

fan
exhaust, in kitchen, 53–54,
112
wall, in dishwashing area, 71
financing, 14–19
fire extinguishers, 62, 86–87, 127
fire insurance, 148–150
fire protection system, 62, 86–87,
126–128
floor slats, bar, 42
flooring
dining area, 93
dishwashing area, 72–73,
111–112
kitchen, 72–73, 111–112
food
frozen, 26
leftover, 137–138
and nutrition, 136–138
purchasing, 130–132
and quality controls, 136
fountain, ice cream soda, 95–99,
193–194
franchising, 18
freezers, 55–58
auxiliary, 85
placement of, 85, 110, 112
storage, 74, 75
types of, 55–56
fryers, deep-, 52–53

garbage cans
in bar, 42
in dishwashing area, 69–70
in kitchen, 63